You Report to Me

Accountability for the Failing Administrative State

David Bernhardt

New York • London

First American edition published in 2023 by Encounter Books, an activity of Encounter for Culture and Education, Inc., a nonprofit, tax-exempt corporation. Encounter Books website address: www.encounterbooks.com

Manufactured in the United States and printed on acid-free paper. The paper used in this publication meets the minimum requirements of ANSI/NISO Z39.48-1992 (R 1997) (*Permanence of Paper*).

FIRST AMERICAN EDITION

Library of Congress Cataloging-in-Publication Data

Names: Bernhardt, David Longly, author.
Title: You report to me : accountability for the failing administrative state / by David Bernhardt.
Description: First American edition. | New York, New York : Encounter Books, 2023. | Includes bibliographical references.
Identifiers: LCCN 2022037062 (print) | LCCN 2022037063 (ebook) ISBN 9781641773300 (hardcover) | ISBN 9781641773317 (ebook)
Subjects: LCSH: United States—Politics and government Public administration—United States
Classification: LCC JK275 .B48 2023 (print) | LCC JK275 (ebook) DDC 320.973—dc23/eng/20221108
LC record available at https://lccn.loc.gov/2022037062
LC ebook record available at https://lccn.loc.gov/2022037063

1 2 3 4 5 6 7 8 9 20 23

Dedication
To my wife, Gena

CONTENTS

INTRODUCTION

On a cold day in December 2018, while serving as the deputy secretary at the U.S. Department of the Interior, I received a directive to report to the Oval Office to meet with the president of the United States. This was the first time I had been called to the Oval Office, and the circumstances were not ideal.

I understood that my direct supervisor at Interior, Secretary Ryan Zinke, was in the process of resigning. The *Washington Post* had reported that Zinke was on the verge of being fired after the department's inspector general made a criminal referral to the Department of Justice. Zinke, on the other hand, had told me that he was going to resign and that it was entirely his own choice. Given these divergent reports, I was unsure what to expect as I headed over to the White House.

When I crossed the threshold into the Oval Office, President Trump looked up from the Resolute Desk and told me to take a seat. A kind host, he asked if I wanted a Coke. He made a few comments regarding his perspective on the current situation with Secretary Zinke, then we briefly discussed the Department of the Interior's priorities. The president appeared interested in our national parks, deregulation, energy activities, mining, outdoor recreation, forest health, and timber management. He then asked my perspective on a few people he was considering as replacements for Zinke. As the discussion wrapped up, he explained, "You're going to be running the ship for a while. Do you have any questions?"*

I cleared my throat, feeling like the backup quarterback about to be thrown into the game. I had many questions, in fact, but I settled on one: "Who do I report to?"

President Trump looked at me quizzically. "You report to me," he said.

"I know that's what the Constitution says," I acknowledged, choosing my words carefully, "but who do I actually report to?"

"You report to me," he repeated. He could not have been more clear. I reported directly to him and to no one else!

Walking back to Interior's massive headquarters on C Street, I recognized that the president's words, if true, meant that my tenure, no matter how short, would be very different from those of the two secretaries I had worked under in the George W. Bush administration. White House staff had played a major role in overseeing the cabinet then, at least at Interior. It was often a lengthy and difficult process for a cabinet secretary to get an idea or an initiative before the president. The process took even longer when the White House staff held a policy view different from that of the cabinet secretary.

I experienced President Bush's staff-dominated agency oversight process when I worked as the counselor to the secretary and later as solicitor (chief legal officer) for the Department of the Interior. During that time, I witnessed Secretary Gale Norton working on energy development issues for months with White House staff before she was able to raise them directly with the president. A similar dynamic played out when I worked closely with Secretary Dirk Kempthorne as he wrestled with the question of whether the polar bear was either a "threatened species" or an "endangered species" under the Endangered Species Act (ESA), an issue that caused significant concern among the president's advisors at the White House.

---

* All conversations are reported from memory, giving my closest approximation of the words spoken.

The U.S. Fish and Wildlife Service, after missing a legal deadline and entering into a settlement agreement in federal court, had committed to an effort to determine whether the polar bear was a threatened species under the terms of the ESA. In enacting that law in 1973, Congress defined what constitutes an "endangered species" or a "threatened species," and then tasked the secretary of the interior with establishing by regulation if a given species falls into one of these categories on the basis of five specific factors. Before making such a determination, the secretary is required to conduct a review of the species' status and take account of efforts made by any state or nation to protect that species. In doing so, the secretary must rely "solely on the best scientific and commercial data available to him."

These legal requirements placed limitations on Secretary Kempthorne's discretion. He was not free to adopt any policy that he or the White House might prefer, but was bound by the law that Congress enacted and by the facts before him. Because of the settlement agreement, he could not wait to develop more data before making his determination. At the same time, he recognized the concerns of the White House. Kempthorne had never had to answer to a boss in his career up to that point, and he agonized over the issue. He was not enthusiastic about making a decision that was inconsistent with the policy perspective of the president or his staff, yet he was determined to make the decision he believed was most appropriate given the law and the facts.

A wide range of entities outside the Fish and Wildlife Service—including other federal agencies, national trade associations, business interests, political leaders, and state governments—were extremely worried that listing the polar bear would trigger an avalanche of new regulations related to global warming under the umbrella of the ESA. After examining the facts and the law, Kempthorne was inclined to list the polar bear as a threatened species. His decision was met with great concern from White House staff who indicated their understanding of President Bush's view to the contrary. After months of dialogue with lower-level White House staff, Kempthorne and I finally met with the chief of staff, Josh Bolton, who made it clear that he wanted the secretary to take ten days to consider alternatives before making a final decision.

Over the next ten days, at Kempthorne's direction, I worked with a team of lawyers and scientists to write a draft alternative rule, accepting the best scientific and commercial data available but rendering a determination that the polar bear was neither an "endangered species" nor a "threatened species" under the law. It was a massive undertaking. The alternative rule we developed was not an approach that Kempthorne or his policy senior advisors found persuasive. At his request, I called the White House deputy chief of staff and informed him that the secretary planned to go forward with listing the polar bear as a threatened species, despite the concerns expressed by the White House staff.

The deputy chief of staff returned with a message from President Bush informing him that while the president continued to support the views of a majority of his advisors, what mattered most to him was that Secretary Kempthorne was comfortable with his own decision. It was exactly what any cabinet secretary should hope to hear from the president—a message essentially saying, "Congress has tasked you with a legal responsibility to carry out the law. I put you in this position. I know you have carefully looked at the matter. Make the decision you think is right."

Relieved to hear it, Kempthorne made what he believed to be the correct decision, though many disagreed. But while the message was great, the White House process for arriving at this point was ridiculous, filled with consternation and staff conflict. Most importantly, Kempthorne appeared to have never had the chance to make his case directly to the president.

Given my experience with presidential oversight during the George W. Bush administration, I was skeptical of the likelihood that I would be communicating directly with President Trump to help him accomplish his agenda. Soon after I took the helm of the Department of the Interior on January 2, 2019, I had occasion to put this approach to the test.

A government shutdown started on December 22, 2018, while I was the deputy secretary. In anticipation of a potential shutdown, informed by Secretary Zinke's policy direction, Interior had formulated a shutdown plan for national parks and other public lands that differed from the approach taken in 2013 by Obama administration officials, who had needlessly and inappropriately shuttered parks and even open-air monuments. The National Park Service went so far as to erect barriers around the World War II Memorial on the National Mall so that visitors couldn't access what is an otherwise open space during the government shutdown. Members of the public were outraged by the Park Service's actions, which resonated as petty and vindictive. Zinke wanted to avoid a similar controversy and maintain public access to the parks throughout a shutdown.

Under Zinke's plan, the parks would be left largely accessible and staffed with law enforcement officers. The gates to the parks would remain open and no entrance fees would be collected. This plan assumed the best of the American people. It assumed that visitors to the parks would largely be responsible and would follow the basic tenet of any backcountry experience: "pack it in, pack it out." While this plan would have worked well for the anticipated short-term shutdown, this particular shutdown lasted over a month, and a few negative consequences appeared after a couple of days. Trash began to pile up in some of the parks, and some visitors misbehaved. Restrooms were either closed or not properly maintained.

The day before Christmas, I witnessed problems firsthand on the National Mall, where many visitors had bought refreshments from the commercial food trucks parked along the mall and left trash that was now overflowing the receptacles and littering the normally pristine lawn. The City of Washington was making an effort to collect some of the trash, but it hardly matched what the dedicated facility staff of the National Park Service did routinely. On Christmas Day, lacking a more sensible option, I secured a Park Service dually pickup truck and took it to the National Mall, collected loads of trash, and hauled it to a dumpster myself. As I filled bag after bag with trash, the wheels in my head were turning. I thought about the hourly facility workers for the parks who were not getting paid. I wondered if there was a way that I could get the facility and maintenance staff paid and back to work, while keeping Zinke's general plan maintaining public access in place. It dawned on me that the Park Service had a reserve of over $250 million from recreation fees. I wondered if that money could be used to pay facilities staff and law enforcement so the parks could be kept clean and safe for visitors during the shutdown.

In previous government shutdowns, some national parks had remained open because particular states agreed to fund the National Park Service's continued operations that were important to the state economy. Normally these transactions were instigated by local park superintendents or local park concessionaires, who approached state political leaders and asked them to fund these federal operations out of the state taxpayers' pockets. In addition to accommodating the interest of the state, this approach also ensured that federal employees who would otherwise be furloughed kept receiving pay. During the shutdown in 2013, for example, Arizona footed the bill to keep the Grand Canyon open, and New York ponied up funds to maintain public access to the Statue of Liberty. Once again, in 2018, superintendents at national parks were trying to get the states to fund the operations, even while the National Park Service was sitting on a mountain of cash that could potentially be used for that very purpose. It seemed to me like extortion.

I examined the relevant law and concluded that the Department of the Interior could almost certainly draw from the previously collected recreation fees to pay for law enforcement, trash cleanup, and facility maintenance during the shutdown. Shortly after I had assumed leadership of the department following the New Year's holiday, the department's lawyers reviewed the matter, agreed with my understanding of the law, and secured approval from the White House Office of Management and Budget to modify our plan. We had a way to ensure that law enforcement and maintenance staff were paid and in place, to keep the parks accessible to the public, and to avoid the controversies of previous shutdowns, without having to shake down the states.

My decision was bound to get media attention, so I wanted to make sure that White House leadership were informed before reading about it in the press. Recalling my first conversation with the president, I picked up the phone and called his receptionist.

"The White House, how may I help you?" answered the president's personal assistant.

"Good morning," I said, "this is Deputy Secretary Bernhardt at Interior. I'm serving as the backup quarterback at the Department of the Interior and I need to get information to the president. He told me I should call him if I needed him to know something, but I don't necessarily need to talk to him. Perhaps you could send me to whomever I'm really supposed to talk to about items like this?"

She laughed and replied, "The president will call you back in a few minutes."

Sure enough, President Trump returned my call a few minutes later. I laid out the situation and told him what I intended to do. The whole process took a few minutes.

Such was my experience with President Trump throughout my tenure. He was accessible when you needed his input, his counsel, or a decision, and he was more than able to contact you whenever he had an issue he wanted to be addressed. His willingness to work and communicate with the executives he had placed in various cabinet agencies was extraordinary. He empowered the department leadership while also ensuring that information flowed directly from the agencies to him. He expected to communicate directly with me, and I was expected to communicate directly with him. As a cabinet secretary, I understood that he expected me to determine how best to execute the priorities he had asked me to focus on within the confines of the law and get to work. He was focused on outcomes and expected his department leadership to advance his policy agenda. In my opinion, he allowed competent leaders to move forward at a much quicker pace than many of his predecessors by selecting a goal, letting them get to work, and not allowing his other staff to get in their way.

President Trump's enabling leadership avoided the massive periods of inactivity that plagued much of my prior experience in the Department of the Interior under President George W. Bush. Far more critically, Trump's expectation that those serving in the executive branch actually report to him reflected a reality about the presidency and his view of it. The Constitution of the United States confers all the executive power of the United States on the president. Only the president has been entrusted by the American people with this power. Therefore, Trump expected that everyone in the executive branch would be working to accomplish the things he committed to the American people that he would do if elected, which he wanted done.

When Congress writes legislation and the president signs it into law, that new law almost always authorizes or directs the head of a cabinet department to carry out some new task. As the department head's responsibilities expand, that person delegates some authority to subordinates to help fulfill the newly assigned tasks. These subordinates are then empowered to exercise this delegated authority, which the department head can withdraw at any time. Each department head serves at the pleasure of the president. Virtually everyone who serves in the executive branch "reports" to the president.

As the nation and the federal administrative agencies have grown, the understanding that every federal employee and every government contractor is acting by a delegation of authority from a department head who serves at the pleasure of the president has drifted out of focus. Those who exercise delegated authority often act as if the executive powers were conferred on them directly, making them not accountable to those who have delegated the authority to them. Such a view is antithetical to representative government and to the Constitution. To the extent accommodated by law, the president's policy preferences, not those of a subordinate, are to guide executive action. A subordinate—whether a political appointee or a career civil servant—can raise issues to superiors, and always has the option of resigning rather than carrying out an action or a policy seen as repugnant. But the subordinate should not act contrary to direction or engage in subterfuge with impunity. Such actions are acts of insubordination.

These pages offer a stress-tested perspective on the challenges faced by political appointees whose attempts to navigate the bureaucratic swamp and drive change are met with the recalcitrance of the administrative state. Because decision-making power has been delegated deep into the bowels of federal agencies, employees often ignore or frustrate the president's policies absent clear direction by political leadership. This book highlights my own experiences with very different approaches to presidential oversight and with executive management of the bureaucracy. I present my views as someone who was initially called to public service as a junior political appointee in the George W. Bush administration and rose through the political ranks over a decade of public service to lead the same cabinet department.

Having spent a great deal of my career in the executive branch, I am gravely concerned that many people who work there believe that they have little need to comply with the written words of the law or the regulations of their agency, or with the policies of the elected president. The leaders of executive agencies, for their part, too often view themselves as little more than figureheads, allowing their agencies to run on autopilot rather than fulfilling their responsibility to supervise employees and hold them accountable to the American people. Both political appointees and career employees have been tasked with upholding the Constitution and the law. It is time for executive branch leaders to exercise meaningful oversight of the bureaucracy and rein in the ever-multiplying agencies of the federal government. Career civil servants must understand that their fidelity to the Constitution and to the American people demands that they carry out the lawful polices of the elected president, whether they find those policies agreeable or not.

I hope that by sharing my perspective I can help Americans appreciate that a representative government requires the political leadership—of both parties—to reassert control of administrative agencies. Our institutions are failing the American people and will continue to do so until accountability is demanded by the public and restored by our political leaders. The following chapters highlight the challenges to representative government and to the rule of law posed by the burgeoning administrative state. I also propose solutions to restore effective leadership and accountability to administrative agencies.

CHAPTER ONE

GROWTH OF THE FEDERAL GOVERNMENT

I first came to Washington, D.C., in 1990 to go to law school and explore my interest in public policy. Fresh out of college, I thought the nation's debt was out of control and the government was way too big. The national debt at the time was $3.2 trillion and I was convinced we were heading for financial disaster. As of 2022, the national debt is a stunning $29 trillion. Despite various efforts to rein in the profligacy, the federal government has continued to spend beyond its means and the size of the government has grown bigger and bigger.

The soaring cost of the federal government is not the only problem; another is its shocking inefficiency. It became obvious to me shortly after I entered the Department of the Interior as a young lawyer in 2001, under Secretary Gale Norton. At the time, I assumed that the secretary could send any letter she wished, to anyone she chose, without jumping over procedural hurdles. Then I learned about something called the surname process, or the clearance process, requiring over a dozen people to sign their approval before the secretary could send a letter. The surname process was not reserved for the secretary's letters. It bogged down everyday department activities, such as publicizing notices and rules in the Federal Register (the official daily publication for rules, proposed rules, and notices of federal agencies and organizations, along with presidential actions). Moving a noncontroversial document from a field office to Washington and then on to the Federal Register could take months. The surname process seemed to me so needlessly time-consuming that one day I set about to learn how it originated.

First off, I found no report or documentation citing the initial impetus for the surname process or indicating that it had been drawn from best practices over the years. Instead, I had to search for the "lore" of how the process came into existence. Basically, I was told that the surname process for documents going to the Federal Register began when a chief of staff to the secretary of the interior in the 1990s had been surprised by a newspaper article about a department action that he didn't like. When the chief of staff asked agency employees where the reporter had found the information, he was told it had been published in the Federal Register. The chief of staff decided that he wanted to review all documents going to the Federal Register from then on. I'm confident that he had no idea what he was setting in motion.

The deputy secretary walked into his office not long after and found him surrounded by dozens of packages. "What are you doing?" he asked.

"Well," replied the chief of staff, "I'm surnaming all of the packages for the Federal Register."

The deputy secretary considered this for a moment. "OK, but you're the chief of staff—a staffer to the secretary," he said. "You don't have anything to do with operations. I need to see those, too."

The deputy secretary then joined the chief of staff in surnaming documents. The deputy secretary's action caught the attention of the department's solicitor, who has to review any document before the deputy secretary can sign it. So he too joined what was becoming the surname process, suddenly reviewing documents he had previously not needed to review, which in turn caught the attention of the assistant secretaries, their staff, and the bureau directors. There's a common reality among government actors: "My boss is looking at a document, so it must be important. If I'm not looking at it, I'm not important." Eventually, dozens of people were involved in the surname process, and supposedly it was all because a chief of staff didn't like a story he'd read in the paper.

The process continued for years, largely unquestioned, and was essentially treated as an internal procedural requirement. No one developed a more efficient process to serve the same purpose. The department staff outside Washington, as well as members of the public who were interested in the publication of particular documents initiating or announcing government decisions, were frustrated by how long it took to get simple notices into the Federal Register.

When I returned to Interior as deputy secretary, I worked to streamline the surname process and other inefficient channels as part of the department's effort to better serve the American people. For example, the review process for environmental impact statements drafted in the field was extraordinarily cumbersome. A team of people in the field would work on a draft document for years before sending it to D.C., where it would then spend months moving from desk to desk. The state directors of the Bureau of Land Management (BLM), which falls within the Department of the Interior, were irritated by how long it took headquarters to review those environmental impact statements. We made the review process more efficient without changing a single environmental standard.

The state BLM directors are members of the Senior Executive Service, a tier in the civil service that is equivalent to generals in the military. They have a lot of authority, so I proposed a procedural change that would place accountability directly on their shoulders. I told the state directors that if they read every environmental impact statement they wanted to submit to the Federal Register, had their lawyers review every document with them, and then put their name on it, they could send the document to me. I would read it myself, and then we could invite everyone in Washington with an interest in it to a meeting or a conference call for discussion. Instead of going through thirty layers of people, we organized a single phone call to deal with any concerns.

As a result, the average length of time it took the BLM to initiate and complete an environmental impact statement dropped dramatically. The change also improved the quality of the impact statements because senior managers actually had to read the documents and defend their team's work product. They were now directly accountable for the environmental impact statements, not forty people whose names were on a surname sheet. By getting people in a room or on a call together, we could also tell whether or not the state directors had read the documents. When they did, those directors realized how poorly drafted and redundant the documents had become. It appeared to me that managers had been forwarding documents to D.C. for years without having taken the time to read them before attaching their name. Most importantly, when decision makers had to be accountable for the documents they provided, the very purpose of the National Environmental Policy Act was better served. Instead of developing environmental impact statements just to stave off litigation, staff began drafting documents that truly informed agency leaders of the potential consequences of proposed actions and set out a reasonable range of alternatives.

In the absence of clear deadlines and effective oversight, routine agency processes can morph into unrecognizable caricatures of government procedure, with little benefit to the public. As the size of government grows ever larger, agencies become further removed from the mission of delivering services for the American people and less responsive to their needs. This chapter traces the historical development of the administrative state into the unwieldy bureaucracy we see today and examines how it has distorted our constitutional model of representative government.

Government Growth and the Administrative State

At the end of the First Congress, the State Department had four employees. Today the department employs roughly 13,000 foreign service members, 11,000 civil service members, and 45,000 additional support staff around the globe. The executive branch as a whole currently employs 2.2 million full-time, part-time, seasonal, and temporary staff. The growth of agency staff reflects the expansion of the federal government's mission, often into areas of the economy and society never imagined by the Framers. Executive branch departments and agencies have swelled from a limited administrative support for the president into a vast bureaucracy endowed with its own authority to regulate the lives of citizens. Executive branch agencies now have the power to promulgate, enforce, and adjudicate their own rules, with limited (or nonexistent) oversight from either Congress or the White House.

The growth and evolution of the administrative state is not just a contemporary phenomenon, but something that has unfolded over the life of our nation. The Civil War inaugurated the first period of significant growth in the federal government. In 1831, it employed 5,837 civilian staff (excluding postal workers); by 1871, the number had grown to 15,344. Wartime needs gave rise to a slew of new responsibilities, such as issuing the first government bonds, levying the first national income tax, and overseeing the first national banking system.[1] The federal government funded the war effort in part by departing from the gold standard and printing paper money, which led to the creation of the U.S. Secret Service in 1865 with the original mission of investigating counterfeit currency. To transport troops and supplies, the Department of War established the United States Military Railroad, which became the world's largest railroad infrastructure system by the war's end.[2] Outfitting the military apparatus resulted in more government contracting as private companies supplied the Union Army with weapons, ammunition, livestock, and materials. During this period, Congress created new federal agencies, including the Department of Agriculture. President Lincoln, in his first annual message to Congress on December 3, 1861, had offered the opinion that "an agricultural and statistical bureau might be profitably organized." The following May, Congress established a department "to acquire and to diffuse amongst the people of the United States useful information on subjects connected with agriculture in the most general and comprehensive sense of that word, and to procure, propagate and distribute amongst the people new and valuable seeds and plants."[3]

The growth of the federal government stalled after the Civil War, but ratcheted up again during the Progressive Era of the late nineteenth and early twentieth centuries. Regulatory initiatives of the time not only increased the size of the federal government but also contributed to the growing power of administrative agencies. The impetus for regulation didn't come only from progressive reformers. During the 1870s, agricultural interests called on federal lawmakers to regulate banks and railroads. Congress responded in 1887 by creating the nation's first regulatory agency, the Interstate Commerce Commission, to regulate railroads and carriers across state lines. Industrialization and immigration contributed to robust wealth creation, but living conditions in many major cities deteriorated and factory environments posed unique hazards to employees. A number of states enacted workers' compensation laws at the close of the nineteenth century to address the problem of accidents in the industrial workplace. In 1906, Congress passed the Federal Meat Inspection Act to protect workers from unsanitary slaughterhouse operations, and the Pure Food and Drugs Act to regulate what the legislation described as "adulterated or misbranded or poisonous or deleterious foods, drugs or medicines, and liquors."

During Woodrow Wilson's presidency, the progressive approach to governance put increasing power in the hands of "experts." Like other progressives, Wilson believed that ordinary citizens lacked the necessary knowledge and wisdom to weigh in on complex matters of policy and law. Democracy "assume[s] a discriminating judgment and a fullness of information on the part of the people touching questions of public policy," Wilson wrote, and in his view the people "do not often possess" that knowledge and judgment.[4] He therefore favored vesting more power in executive agencies staffed by experts and insulated from interference by an increasingly diverse electorate.

In *Constitutional Government in the United States*, Wilson elaborated on a departure from the Founders' view of the constitutional framework, with its principle of popular sovereignty tempered by checks and balances, in favor of a Darwinian concept in structure and practice. Wilson viewed the U.S. Constitution as a "living thing" that changes with society over time, "modified by its environment, necessitated by its tasks, shaped to its functions by the sheer pressure of life."[5] The constitutional separation of powers between three branches of government, he suggested, could adapt to the evolving role of administrative agencies.

In "The Study of Administration," Wilson argued that experts should be tasked with managing government administration away from political influence. "The ideal for us," he wrote, "is a civil service cultured and self-sufficient enough to act with vigor, and yet so intimately connected with popular thought by means of elections and constant public counsel, as to find arbitrariness or class spirit quite out of the question."[6] Wilson predicted that a "technically schooled civil service will presently become indispensable." He did acknowledge that "a great many very thoughtful persons" were concerned that this approach to governance would engender "an offensive class—a distinct, semi-corporate body with sympathies divorced from those of a progressive, free-spirited people and with hearts narrowed to the meanness of bigoted officialdom."[7] From my own perspective, those "thoughtful" critics were far closer to the mark than Wilson in foreseeing the results of rule by an insulated bureaucracy.

The Wilson administration together with Congress laid the groundwork for the administrative state and its regulatory apparatus. The Progressive Era introduced the structure of independent agencies, designed to operate with some degree of autonomy from political influence. The Federal Reserve Act of 1913 established the Federal Reserve System and implemented federal regulation of the banking industry. The following year, the Federal Trade Commission (FTC) was founded and the Clayton Act strengthened the FTC's antitrust enforcement powers.

During the 1920s, the growth of government administration again slowed and even receded.[8] Then the stock market crash of 1929 and the Great Depression gave rise to the New Deal (1933–1939), through which President Franklin Roosevelt and Congress effectively seized control of the financial system and tasked the administrative bureaucracy with managing much of American society in ways not previously contemplated. The New Deal brought a fresh wave of expansion in federal agencies. The Securities Acts of 1933 and 1934, for instance, set up the Securities and Exchange Commission to regulate the securities markets. The National Labor Relations Board and the Federal Communications Commission were also created during this period.

The administration of President Lyndon Johnson launched a variety of new programs under the Great Society agenda. President

Richard Nixon followed up by creating a series of new federal agencies, including the Environmental Protection Agency, the Consumer Product Safety Commission, the National Highway Traffic Safety Administration, and the Occupational Safety and Health Administration. While it was primarily Democratic administrations that drove the growth of the bureaucracy in the early twentieth century, Republicans also contributed to its expansion in the second half of the century and into the next.

Today's administrative state is made up of a complex combination of executive branch agencies and independent federal agencies. Government also operates through outside contracting and grant making, which obscures the true size and scope of the administrative state. In addition, there are congressionally chartered foundations set up as nonprofit entities for the purpose of supporting federal agency missions. These foundations have become their own lobbying force, largely funded by corporate and private donations, and they add yet another layer of complexity to the administrative swamp.

Growth of Agency Power

The Founders intended to create a government that operates by the consent of the governed. They designed a system in which the people elect representatives to Congress to promote their interests by legislation. The people also elect a president to execute the nation's laws. The judiciary, appointed and confirmed by the people's elected representatives, interprets the nation's laws and aims to ensure that Congress and the executive branch act within their legal authority. As James Madison cautioned in *Federalist* no. 47, the accumulation of all powers in a single authority is "the very definition of tyranny."[9] The Founders therefore distributed powers among three branches of government, with a system of checks and balances, so that no one person could become all-powerful.

The idea of a separation of powers was central to the drafting of the U.S. Constitution. Under this doctrine, three powers—executive, legislative, judicial—must be kept distinct in order to restrain government overreach and abuses of power. The growth of the administrative state since the early twentieth century not only brought a vast increase in the number of federal agencies, but also, over time, had the result of shifting legislative and judicial authority into administrative agencies that hold executive authority.

This expansion of power in executive agencies has been facilitated by changes in attitudes toward two key practices by which the legislature and the judiciary have essentially ceded much of their constitutional authority to the executive branch. The first of these is delegation, in which the legislature gives broad grants of rulemaking authority to agencies of the executive branch. The leaders of those agencies, in turn, delegate decision-making authority down to low-level employees, who often exercise it with little oversight. The other key practice is judicial deference, in which courts defer to agency interpretations of statutory language in their regulatory actions. These two practices allow administrative agencies to wield increasing power in a way that is insulated from the people's elected representatives. Consequently, the American people are being hindered from influencing policy through the ballot box.

Restoring governance that reflects the will of the American people requires at least one of three things to occur: 1) Congress must craft legislation more clearly and take its oversight responsibilities more seriously; 2) the political leadership in executive agencies must affirmatively reassert their proper role in the constitutional framework to prevent employees from acting with little political accountability; or 3) the courts must become more skeptical toward an executive agency's assertion of authority where Congress has not been clear in its intent. In the following chapters, we will take a closer look at how the administrative state has eroded political accountability and how renewed leadership can give the American people their voice back again.

CHAPTER TWO

UNACCOUNTABLE BUREAUCRACY

In December 2016, I was immersed in the effort to develop a transition plan for the Department of the Interior. The president-elect had recently announced has nominee to serve as secretary of the interior, Ryan Zinke, a Montana native, a former Navy Seal, and a one-term congressman. After meeting with him for the first time, I looked forward to his confirmation. My positive view about the upcoming administration, however, wasn't mirrored by a lot of the Washington establishment—a disparity I saw as a really good thing. In my opinion, the nation needed a president willing to drive change. But throughout the fall, numerous Republicans "in the know" spent a great deal of time explaining to me that there was no way for then-candidate Trump to beat Hillary Clinton. These Republicans were in a state of surprise in December 2016, and their Democratic counterparts were in a state of shock and despondency.

That despondency is a part of life in D.C. during a presidential transition, but what was happening in the halls of government agencies was troubling. I was informed that political appointees in the

Obama administration had actually encouraged their career staff to dress in black to mourn Hillary Clinton's election loss. This behavior was completely inconsistent with the graciousness that President George W. Bush had demanded of his political appointees during the transition to the Obama administration. Even more ominous were the many news reports that began to appear in the media with headlines such as "Downtrodden in D.C.: Federal employees are in tears with the reality of working with Donald Trump." That particular story in the *National Post* of Canada reported that "a funeral atmosphere had taken hold in government offices in the U.S. Capitol where numerous federal employees describe mournful, even tearful, scenes among dejected co-workers commiserating about Donald Trump's impending presidency." Employees were "wondering how they can make life more difficult for him." Some were planning to leave, but others intended to resist, in some cases by "executing very slowly."[1] Bloomberg similarly reported that career staff had "found ways to obstruct, slow down or simply ignore their new leader, the president."[2] One federal employee boasted to the *Washington Post* that we would "see the bureaucrats using time to their advantage" to frustrate President Trump's policies.[3]

I found these reports to be extremely problematic. Anyone who joins the career civil service signs up to work for whomever the American people elect to be our nation's president, whether or not the people's choice reflects their personal policy views. My concern about the prospect of resistance raised by some members of the civil service as the Obama administration wound down prompted me to begin my service as deputy secretary by sending an all-employee email throughout the Department of the Interior (see Appendices) that included the following perspective:

> I believe each of us choose to come to the Department because we believe in serving the people. We love the Department's mission.

We want to make it even better. We maintain those values even when our conclusions differ. We can have healthy disagreements. However, ultimately, it is the policymaker's job, to the extent they have discretion, to exercise that discretion in accord with the administration's view. This is because each President represents the will of the people, until the next one is sworn in.

Over the next few years, the vast majority of employees at Interior understood and carried out their duties in an exemplary manner. But sadly, the number of staff who chose to "resist" was exponentially higher than in my first tour of duty in the department under President George W. Bush.

During that time, the benefit of a neutral, expert civil service for the elected administration—and for the nation—was ingrained in me: political appointees in the executive branch can and should collaborate with the members of the career civil service to carry out the law and bring about the president's preferred policy outcomes, consistent with the law. I had occasion to test that principle a few days into my tenure as director of the Interior Department's Office of Congressional and Legislative Affairs. Two senior members of Secretary Gale Norton's management team instructed me to begin the process of reassigning the department's legislative counsel—a career member of the civil service tasked with managing, clearing, and revising all of Interior's testimony to Congress—out of my office, because they considered her too liberal. After listening to their request, I decided that the best thing I could do was meet with the legislative counsel myself and decide if we would be able to work together.

I asked her into my office the next day. A consummate professional, she took a seat across the desk from me and waited to hear the reason for the meeting. After some small talk, I asked her only one critical question: "As a public attorney, who is your client?"

"The secretary of the interior," she replied without skipping a beat.

"Do you think you can fairly represent her?" I asked.

"Of course," she said.

I believed her, and nothing more needed to be discussed. It was clear to me that she understood her duty as a civil servant. She was a competent lawyer who worked for her client, the secretary of the interior. Regardless of which party won the election, it was her job as legislative counsel to ensure that the legal and policy interests of the secretary were represented in her work. I concluded that I could work with her. Without further ado, I went back to senior management and told them that she would be staying on in her role.

The wisdom of my decision to push back on a knee-jerk suggestion from senior management was validated many times in the next several years. The legislative counsel's knowledge, experience, and assistance were instrumental in my office's success on a host of issues. She took a professional approach to her work with political appointees, perhaps best demonstrated during our time working together on a 2001 policy proposal affecting the Arctic National Wildlife Refuge (ANWR). I had asked her to draft legislative language allowing for oil and gas development in a 1.6-million-acre zone within the boundaries of the 19-million-acre ANWR. The question of whether Congress should enact such legislation had been batted around for decades. Nevertheless, the most relevant document examining potential ANWR development at the time was a dated environmental impact statement (EIS) from 1987.

One afternoon, while the legislative counsel was working on the ANWR language, I noticed that she had highlighted her copy of the EIS in two different colors. "That's pretty interesting," I said, gesturing toward the color-coded text.

"Well, look," she shrugged, "every four to eight years a crew of you come in and I have to do the same damn thing with this report. Finally, I just highlighted the Democratic talking points in one color and the Republican talking points in another so that I can go back and forth."

This approach epitomized how the civil service should operate. The legislative counsel didn't play for one team or the other, but endeavored to serve all Americans with her specialized knowledge and expertise. Equally important, she taught me the value of collaboration between skilled career staff and political appointees for maximizing an administration's success during its limited time in office.

In my second tour at the Department of the Interior, dedicated and attentive civil servants of the U.S. Park Police impressed me with their sense of duty, particularly during the summer of 2020 and through the final days of the Trump administration. The death of George Floyd sparked protests across the country that presented big challenges for Interior, which oversees our national parks and monuments. In particular, the Park Police, working with threadbare resources by comparison with other federal law enforcement entities, found themselves embroiled in controversy over the clearing of protesters from Lafayette Square, a public park just north of the White House graced with statues and monuments. Over a weekend, groups associated with the likes of Antifa had attacked officers who were policing the protest. Some even threw firebombs through the basement windows of the historic St. John's Episcopal Church, a short walk across the park from the White House. The Park Service made the decision to install fencing around Lafayette Square to help protect the officers who had been under attack and to guard the statues and monuments from vandalism. Soon after Park Police had cleared the square so the contractors could install the fencing, President Trump decided to walk from the White House to St. John's, igniting a media firestorm and allegations that the Park Police had cleared protesters from the area just to provide the president with a photo opportunity in front of the church.

While the controversy swirled, various public statements and media reports claimed that Attorney General Bill Barr was in charge of the Park Police operation, but this in fact wasn't the case. The leadership of the Park Police clearly understood their jurisdiction, and they understood that they had my support to push back against anyone who might ask them to take an action outside their jurisdiction.

In the aftermath, Democratic members of Congress wasted no time in boosting the media narrative and criticizing the Park Police's response to the protests in Lafayette Square. The inspector general's report on the incident, issued a year later, cleared the Park Police from allegations of collusion with the White House.[4] The report found that Park Police had acted lawfully to clear the area of protesters in order to install protective fencing around the historic site. While the report found some communication problems between the assisting law enforcement agencies at the scene, everything else about the department's response—and that of the Park Police—had moved according to plan. The partisan attacks and the media's continued drive of a false portrayal of the Park Police's actions stirred up a frenzy that led to vicious attacks on the honorable character of the men and women of the Park Police.

Interestingly, the SWAT team that the Park Police used to clear Lafayette Square was the same SWAT team deployed on January 6, 2021, to respond to the lawlessness at the Capitol and protect members of Congress. I believe the team fired over two thousand pepper balls that day. In one of my final speeches as secretary, I thanked the Park Police for their distinction and devotion to duty, noting how remarkable their service was on January 6 when some of the same members of Congress they protected had called them thugs and berated them all summer long. Their actions said everything about the honor and commitment of the law enforcement officials and civil servants in the U.S. Park Police.

The protests raged on during the summer of 2020, and so did the Covid-19 pandemic. In the face of the unexpected coronavirus outbreak, a remarkable contingent of public health experts worked with the Department of the Interior to manage access to our national parks and facilities during a time when nature and the great outdoors provided safe recreation and enjoyment to so many Americans.

The George W. Bush administration had created a pandemic plan in 2005 after the SARS epidemic. While serving as solicitor in 2007, I received a copy of the Pandemic Influenza Plan for Interior, setting out how the department would protect the health and safety of employees; maintain essential functions and services during events that resulted in significant and sustained absenteeism; support federal, state, and local responses to a pandemic; and communicate with stakeholders. As Covid-19 spread widely, I anticipated that the federal government would largely ask everyone to follow the existing plan. I did not anticipate that the president would initiate a fifteen-day effort to Stop the Spread. This approach told me that he had established public health as the primary policy goal over all other concerns for the time being. I was not convinced that this policy elevation was actually based on risk, but I would dutifully work to carry out the priority. Fortunately for the Department of the Interior, the U.S. surgeon general has long assigned a cadre of public health officers to the U.S. National Park Service. These officers had performed a variety of functions over the years, such as checking water quality to ensure the safety of employees and visitors to our national parks. The Park Service assembled a detail of these public health experts to be part of an emergency response management unit for the department.

I was appreciative, to say the least. Their presence meant I had experts that my leadership team and I could engage with about the developing science and weigh their insight into the department's response. They provided me with information and input on virtually every decision we made regarding the pandemic. That said, I also made clear from the beginning that, while I respected their opinion, any final decisions on the department's pandemic response were ultimately my responsibility. They wholeheartedly agreed, and then worked with my staff and the deputy secretary to develop a guide for the department's pandemic response. It provided a set of standards by which department staff and public health experts would evaluate our activities and facilities, like indoor theater spaces, and decide on a case-by-case basis whether and how to limit access while continuing to allow Americans to enjoy the great outdoors. As circumstances evolved, staff could reassess conditions by the same standards and reopen particular areas as appropriate through an up-front mechanism. Many people wanted us to close all the national parks and public lands to visitors, but the information given to the department by the public health officers did not lead to a conclusion that such an action was necessary. I believed, moreover, that access to parks and other open spaces during this crisis would be beneficial to the American people and to their mental health.

The department was very fortunate to have those public health experts on hand at the Park Service. Shortly before I left the department, we held an award ceremony to thank them. Their guidance was crucial in helping us ensure that our actions were consistent with the available science as understood at the time. I will always appreciate the role they played in informing our decisions. As it turned out, our national parks, wildlife refuges, and public lands provided respite to millions of Americans during a dark and challenging time.

Those model civil servants stand in stark contrast to the agency employees who chose to "resist" the Trump administration's policy endeavors. Efforts to undermine the collaborative relationship between the civil service and political appointees, whatever the reason, fundamentally frustrate the will of the American people. I don't believe our form of government can function if a large majority of the civil service view themselves as only obligated to serve the elected leadership of one political party. I equally believe that the failure of the elected political leadership to do the hard work of demanding accountability when confronted with such "resistance" jeopardizes representative government. The rest of this chapter aims to shed light on the evolution of the civil service from a corps of neutral experts, as originally conceived, into the insulated and occasionally hostile body we see today.

The Civil Service and Removal Protections

United States Code § 2101 defines the federal civil service as consisting of all unelected "positions in the executive, judicial, and legislative branches of the Government of the United States, except positions in the uniformed services." In the late eighteenth century, the federal civil service was very small—the State Department, as noted earlier, was originally staffed by four employees—and federal workers were seldom removed from office. Removals of federal employees increased during the nineteenth century when politically aligned patronage appointments became commonplace, most notably during President Andrew Jackson's administration (1829–1837).

Patronage appointments gave rise to what historians refer to as the spoils system, whereby presidents rewarded their loyal supporters with appointments to government positions. New presidents would remove their predecessor's appointees and replace them with their own supporters, leading many federal jobs to be filled on the basis of political connections rather than competence. President Jackson "claimed to be purging the corruption, laxity, and arrogance that came with long tenure, and restoring the opportunity for government service to the citizenry at large through 'rotation in office,'" as Daniel Feller put it.[5] But the American public came to view the spoils system as an impediment to reliable government services. Appointments based on loyalty rather than skill prevented agency staff from developing institutional expertise and undermined agency performance. After a discontented federal job seeker assassinated President James Garfield in 1881, President Chester Arthur heeded the public call to end the spoils system.

The Pendleton Civil Service Reform Act of 1883 replaced patronage appointments with a merit-based selection process that allowed individuals to gain federal employment through their performance on examinations. The Pendleton Act also barred agencies from firing employees on account of political activities outside the job, but it did not otherwise restrict the president from firing federal employees. The law focused almost entirely on the hiring process, because civil service reformers feared that removal protections would make it difficult for the government to fire poor performers. George William Curtis, the president of the National Civil Service Reform League and one of the drafters of the Pendleton Act, argued:

> Having annulled all reason for the improper exercise of the power of dismissal, we hold that it is better to take the risk of occasional injustice from passion and prejudice, which no law or regulation can control, than to seal up incompetency, negligence, insubordination, insolence, and every other mischief in the service, by requiring a virtual trial at law before an unfit or incapable clerk can be removed.[6]

In the late nineteenth and early twentieth centuries, members of the competitive civil service gained increasing workforce benefits, including workers' compensation and retirement annuities. Through executive orders signed by President William McKinley and President William Howard Taft, and subsequently codified into law in the Lloyd–La Follette Act of 1912, competitive service employees also gained limited procedural protections against removal. The new procedures were intended to prevent politically motivated firing by ensuring that supervisors in the executive branch could fire civil service employees only for legitimate reasons. These procedural safeguards compelled managers to document nonpolitical reasons for a removal, but if the agency determined that the removal was appropriate, the employee could not appeal.

The right to appeal a dismissal began with the Veterans Preference Act of 1944, long after the demise of the spoils system. This law required federal agencies to give hiring preference to veterans, besides allowing veterans—and only veterans—to appeal a removal to the Civil Service Commission. This provision was a means to prevent agencies from circumventing the hiring preference through pretextual firing.

The broader civil service didn't get dismissal appeals until John F. Kennedy's administration in the 1960s. By that point, veterans made up a considerable portion of the federal workforce. Giving removal appeals only to them came to seem arbitrary. President Kennedy therefore signed Executive Order 10987, requiring agencies to allow nonveterans to appeal their dismissal too. The civil service protections that Americans widely believe were instituted to bring an end to the spoils system actually came about eight decades after the transition to a professional civil service.

The Civil Service Reform Act of 1978 (CSRA) subsequently codified federal employee removal appeals while dividing the Civil Service Commission's responsibilities across several agencies. Federal employees can now challenge their dismissal in four main ways.

Most federal employees can appeal dismissals to the Merit Systems Protection Board. An MSPB administrative law judge (ALJ)— a type of federal administrative adjudicator—will hold trial-like proceedings to determine if the employee deserved to be fired, or if the punishment should be reduced to something less severe, such as a suspension. An employee who loses before the ALJ can appeal to the three presidentially appointed members of the MSPB. Full appeals take an average of nine months.

Alternatively, employees who are part of the majority of the federal workforce represented by a union can work with the union to file a grievance. An arbitrator will then hold trial-like proceedings to decide if they should keep their job. Unions help select these arbitrators, who usually either vacate the removal entirely or downgrade it to a suspension. The arbitration process typically takes several months, and in some cases over a year.

Employees can also file a complaint with the Equal Employment Opportunity Commission (EEOC) alleging that their agency illegally discriminated against them. This triggers an internal agency investigation. If a determination is made that the dismissal was legitimate, the employee can appeal to the EEOC. The process is very long, taking an average of nearly three years if employees ask for a hearing before an administrative judge.

Congress originally created EEOC appeals to combat discrimination in the federal workforce. That was a noble and important goal, but the system has the potential for abuse in the federal government. Filing a complaint—even a completely meritless one—immediately makes holding an employee accountable risky. It allows the employee to allege they were really fired for discriminatory reasons or in retaliation for bringing EEOC charges, which effectively puts their supervisor in the hot seat. Since the EEOC procedure is lengthy, bringing a complaint can freeze the removal process for an extended period. Complaints also give employees leverage: they can offer to drop the complaint if their agency stops trying to remove them from their job. This all costs employees nothing, since agencies cover the expense of the investigation.

Federal employees who suspect they might get reprimanded or fired often file meritless EEOC complaints preemptively. I have seen employees level radical EEOC claims even in the most obviously justifiable of personnel actions. Federal employees file about fifteen thousand discrimination complaints a year. In 2019, the EEOC found that actual discrimination occurred in fewer than two hundred of these cases.[7] EEOC complaints have essentially become a form of de facto employment protection.

Finally, employees can also file a complaint with the Office of Special Counsel alleging whistleblower retaliation or another prohibited personnel practice. As with EEOC complaints, Congress had very good intentions when it passed whistleblower protection laws. No federal employee should ever be fired for exposing wrongdoing. But poor-performing employees also know that discipline and termination are legally fraught if they become "whistleblowers." Some employees who fear removal make meritless or trivial "protected disclosures" just to get whistleblower protections. The Office of Special Counsel reports that it substantiates only about 3 percent of whistleblower reports.

Insulation of the Civil Service

The civil service reformers envisioned a merit-based, accountable civil service, but the protections against discriminatory firing give managers the impression (and at times the reality) that dismissing a poor-performing federal employee is very difficult, if not impossible. The Merit Systems Protection Board itself has long acknowledged that "many supervisors believe it is simply not worth the effort to attempt to remove federal employees who cannot or will not perform adequately."[8] An Office of Personnel Management study from 1999 concluded that only 8 percent of civil service managers with poor-performing employees even attempted to discipline or fire them. Of those who did, 78 percent reported that their efforts had no effect.[9] A recent MSPB survey revealed that few supervisory staff (career or political) were confident they could remove a problem employee if they tried.[10]

In short, agencies rarely try to fire problematic employees. OPM data for 2020 show that agencies dismissed fewer than four thousand out of 1.6 million tenured civil service employees that year. The federal government now employs an insulated civil service lacking accountability. Federal employees know that dismissing them for all but the worst offenses is prohibitively difficult. One result is that career employees can often pursue their own policy goals without repercussions. The ability of career civil servants to advance their own agendas and frustrate policy initiatives they dislike has been well documented.[11]

The problem of employees choosing to follow their own policy objectives is exacerbated by the political leanings of the federal bureaucracy. Despite nonpartisan merit hiring, federal employees lean to the left overall, as numerous studies have shown. In 2021, for example, researchers at Northwestern University and the University of California at Berkeley found twice as many registered Democrats as registered Republicans in the civil service. In the Senior Executive Service—the most senior federal managers— registered Democrats outnumbered Republicans by nearly three to one.[12] A more recent study by researchers at the University of Pennsylvania and the University of Southern California showed that career federal employees gave political donations predominantly to left-leaning candidates.[13]

The upshot is that the federal bureaucracy is dominated by ideological liberals who their supervisors believe are almost impossible to fire. I personally believe that the vast majority of these liberal civil servants set aside their policy views to serve their country honorably. I know many career employees who did not agree with President Trump's policies yet faithfully implemented them. But employees with less integrity could and did work to stymie policies they disagreed with. Simply put, intransigent career employees are a significant impediment to a Republican president's ability to implement the agenda that he (or she) campaigned on.

James Sherk served with me in the Trump administration, working as a White House advisor. Since he left the White House, he has been the director of the America First Policy Institute's Center for American Freedom, where I serve as the chair. One of the Center's projects was interviewing former administration officials to document how career staff interacted with President Trump's appointees. James reported some of the project's findings in "Tales from the Swamp," from which he has permitted me to quote extensively (with minor adjustments in phrasing).[14]

In 2016, an Asian-American advocacy group asked the Department of Justice (DOJ) to investigate Yale's and other Ivy League universities' admissions practices. The advocates suspected racial discrimination against Asian-Americans in violation of the Civil Rights Act. The Educational Opportunities Section (EOS) within the DOJ Civil Rights Division exists to investigate such complaints. However, the complaint languished because EOS career staff did not support the case. Winning would effectively prohibit racial preferences in higher education—racial preferences that they supported.

In 2018, political appointees directed the career deputy who ran the EOS to oversee the Yale investigation and move it along. The career deputy did so, despite philosophically disagreeing with the case. The investigation still took much longer than usual, despite being straightforward. Finally, after two years of investigating, the DOJ uncovered strong evidence of racial discrimination against Caucasians and even stronger evidence of discrimination against Asian-Americans. Political appointees personally drafted a racial discrimination complaint against Yale—a task that junior career lawyers would typically handle.

DOJ then needed to assemble a team to pursue the Yale racial discrimination case. Political appointees asked EOS to provide eight lawyers to work on the case. The career staff refused outright, telling political appointees that none of them would work on it. Political appointees subsequently learned that senior career lawyers warned junior employees not to help the Trump Administration with the case or their careers would suffer. DOJ ultimately had to assemble a team from outside EOS, primarily made up of employees borrowed from the DOJ Civil Division, the U.S. Attorney's Office in Connecticut (where Yale is located), and the Civil Rights Division's front office. DOJ had clear evidence of racial discrimination at Yale and a clear legal theory, but no EOS career lawyers would work on the case because it did not support their worldview.

———

DOJ Civil Rights Division career staff were similarly unwilling to protect conscience rights. The bipartisan Church Amendments broadly prohibit hospitals from forcing nurses to participate in abortions. However, only the Department of Justice can enforce these rights—nurses cannot sue on their own behalf. DOJ Civil Rights Division career staff opposed the Church Amendments and would not work on cases enforcing them. To bring cases enforcing conscience protections, the Trump Administration needed to rely almost entirely on political appointees. Civil Rights Division career staff would not enforce this law that they opposed.

———

Career NLRB lawyers would only present precedents supporting their preferred case resolution. While they would accurately summarize prior cases, the staff appeared to be—or at least pretended to be—almost incapable of presenting cases that undercut their preferred position. Several NLRB subdivisions never presented arguments supporting the employer's position— only reasons why the union should prevail. This made evaluating cases very difficult. NLRB political appointees had to do their own research to understand both sides of the legal arguments. Career staff would then fiercely object if political appointees rejected their recommendations. One senior career employee frequently cried when her recommendations were overruled. Unfortunately, this behavior was not atypical. Many other agencies reported that career staff selectively presented only legal precedents that supported their preferred position. A subsequent FOIA request documented NLRB career staff celebrating (over agency emails no less) how their self-described "resistance" had stymied the Trump appointees' policies.

Department of Education (ED) career staff concealed documents that political appointees wanted to review. Under the Obama Administration, ED alleged that several for-profit colleges were effectively defrauding students. The Department subsequently denied these colleges access to federal student aid. This bankrupted them almost immediately, as they lost significant numbers of students and associated revenues. The schools had no opportunity to defend against these charges before going under. After President Trump took office, political appointees asked to review the evidence that justified this administrative death penalty. Career employees refused to turn over the internal documents. They provided various excuses, such as claiming that they did not have the data anymore or that the people involved had left. However, ED subsequently had to turn over this evidence during a lawsuit. Career employees then promptly produced memos summarizing the Department's evidence against the for-profit schools. Those memos showed that the Department had a weak case. This intransigence was very frustrating to ED political appointees. ED career staff had precisely the information they were looking for all along, but concealed it until legally required to disclose it.

————

Career employees in the EPA Office of General Counsel (OGC) routinely failed to keep political appointees informed about significant cases. OGC would have weekly staff meetings about agency litigation. EPA political appointees would subsequently double-check with Department of Justice (DOJ) lawyers and find out the career staff were not providing updates for critical cases. The career employees were not telling political appointees about significant cases EPA was involved in or the legal arguments EPA was making. Staff omissions were so frequent and significant that political appointees resorted to regularly checking PACER to see what was happening.

————

Career employees at the Department of Labor consistently told political appointees they could not take actions that were in fact within their legal discretion. One career employee repeatedly told political appointees that they could not issue Direct Final Rules (DFR)—a method of issuing rules without going through notice-and-comment proceedings. On the first day of the Biden Administration, DOL used a DFR to rescind internal regulations governing DOL's rulemaking process. That DFR was signed by a career staffer who repeatedly told Trump political appointees, "you can never do a DFR."

————

NLRB career employees "misstated" the dates the agency's union contract could be reopened for renegotiation. Had political appointees taken their word for it, the deadline would have passed, and they would have been stuck with the contract negotiated under the Obama Administration. Fortunately, they double-checked the contract themselves, found career staff gave them the wrong dates, and reopened the contract.

———

DOJ sought to protect the rights of girls and young women to compete on a level playing field in high school and college sports. The Civil Rights Division supported parents in Connecticut suing to prevent biological males who identified as women from unfairly competing against girls in track meets and an Idaho law barring biological males from competing against women. The Division's career staff opposed these efforts, and political appointees performed all related legal work. So while the Civil Rights Division has over 400 lawyers and professional employees, it had only about a dozen lawyers—primarily political appointees—willing to work on certain issues. Political appointees believed these limitations significantly impaired the Division's effectiveness.

———

Some career lawyers at the National Labor Relations Board flat-out refused to draft decisions whose conclusions they disagreed with. Political appointees got the impression these career lawyers were almost daring the political appointees to dismiss them. The lawyers made it clear they would then claim the political appointees were not following the law and assert whistleblower protections. The political appointees were indeed seeking to change existing NLRB precedents—but this is well within the NLRB's authority. Under President Obama, the NLRB overruled a cumulative 4,500 years of existing precedents. Nonetheless, these career lawyers would not write decisions overturning administrative precedents they supported.

—

A DOL enforcement agency has a subcomponent whose only job is to write regulatory and policy documents. The unit has approximately 10 to 15 career employees at any given time. In the fall of 2017, political appointees requested a status update on a draft proposed rule. The unit had been working on this rule since the start of the Trump Administration. It was a department priority and this unit's primary responsibility during this period. Career staff reported the draft would not be complete until March 2018. Political appointees asked for the draft before the end of the year. Career staff said that pace was impossibly burdensome and would drive staff to quit. Political appointees subsequently calculated that the staff's proposed pace amounted to each career employee writing one line of text per day. Appointees estimated that a competent private-sector lawyer could complete the draft in two to three weeks. Political appointees subsequently gave up on these career staff and wrote many policy documents themselves.

—

All politically sensitive regulations at the Education Department (ED) had to be written by political appointees. Career employees assigned to produce drafts of these regulations would come back with "completely unusable" drafts that either diverged significantly from Department priorities or would never withstand judicial review. So political appointees had to do it themselves. For example, the Education Department's Title IX rule (providing due process when students are accused of sexual misconduct) was drafted almost entirely by political appointees. Career involvement served only to preview the arguments that opponents of the rule would eventually make in the courts and the public sphere once the rule was published.

—

The U.S. Department of Agriculture (USDA) participated in the administration-wide effort to reduce the National Environmental

Policy Act (NEPA) regulatory burden. The administration wanted
to clarify that the federal government simply guaranteeing a loan
is not a "major federal action" subject to a burdensome NEPA
review. The Council on Environmental Quality (CEQ) was
working on the rule and turned to USDA to write that section.
USDA career staff included attorneys and experts who were
highly competent and well versed in these issues. But when it
came time to draft the rule, these career staff somehow could not
produce anything that political appointees thought passed legal
muster. Career staff spent 30 days creating unusable work product
for an administration priority. Ultimately political appointees had
to write the analysis themselves. It took political appointees 10
days to do the work and then turn it over to CEQ. USDA political
appointees found it "unbelievable" that capable career employees
did such shoddy work.

Senior leaders at the Department of Justice wanted to issue
guidance clarifying that the law allowed states that modified
voting policies during the COVID-19 pandemic to return to
their pre-pandemic practices afterward. Career lawyers in the
Civil Rights Division instead argued that federal law makes
voting policies a one-way ratchet: once states expand them, they
cannot revert to previous practices. Political appointees directed
a career attorney to write a memo providing legal justification
for the guidance. That career lawyer accepted the assignment.
But his memo argued against the policy and said it lacked any
legal justification. The project had to be assigned to political
appointees, who found solid legal arguments justifying the memo.
In a 6-to-3 decision, the Supreme Court subsequently held that
federal law does not make voting policies a one-way ratchet—
precisely the position the career lawyer said lacked any legal
support.

———

President Trump issued a federal hiring freeze shortly after taking office. A few months later, political appointees at the HHS reviewed several HHS advisory committees' HR records. They noticed that many committee members initially had starting dates after the hiring freeze. HHS career staff had crossed out the initial hiring dates with a sharpie pen, writing in January 19, 2017, instead—the day before President Trump's inauguration.

———

An Interior Department coal plant inspector planned to shut down a mine that employed approximately 30 workers for three months. The mine violated technical Interior protocols, but this paperwork violation did not create any health or safety risks. The mine had the right to appeal and remedy the violation without penalty—keeping the mine open and letting workers keep their incomes through the Thanksgiving and Christmas holidays. Political appointees directed the inspector to allow the mine to stay open while remedying the violation. However, the inspector refused to obey these directives and persisted in driving to the mine to order it to shut down. The inspector only stood down after the Deputy Secretary was patched into a call with the inspector and ordered him to turn his Prius around and let the mine stay open and the workers keep their jobs!

———

In 2020 the USDA wanted to reinstate regulations reforming the school lunch program. USDA had published regulations in 2018 giving states more flexibility to meet the school lunch program's nutritional standards. This rule allowed states to serve meals that students would actually want to eat. Opponents sued, and in April 2020 a federal district court judge ruled against USDA on procedural grounds. The court held that the agency had the authority to make those changes but had made mistakes in complying with notice-and-comment requirements.

If a court invalidates a rule for procedural reasons, the agency can bring it back in effect by redoing the rulemaking process and fixing the procedural defect. The first step is to republish the proposal in the Federal Register—this time providing adequate notice of the intended final policy. Putting this notice together is a ministerial task; the agency has previously done almost all the work of creating the rule. It must simply republish that proposal with only a slight modification. The task generally takes only a few days. After the district court ruled against USDA, political appointees directed the Food and Nutrition Service (FNS) to publish a revised notice in the Federal Register. Career FNS staff pretended they did not know how to put the notice together. The task should have been done by the summer. Instead, hostile staff dragged the process out for months. Political appointees were preoccupied with the coronavirus pandemic and did not have the bandwidth to drive the career FNS team. As a result, the notice was not submitted to the Federal Register in time for USDA to redo the regulatory process, and the rule was never issued. FNS career staff ran out the clock on the rulemaking process and killed a policy they opposed.

The same FNS career staff who dragged their feet on this ministerial task rapidly implemented significant policy changes for the Biden Administration. In the first year of the Biden Administration, FNS expanded food stamp benefits by 30 percent while weakening work requirements for able-bodied adults.

———————

A striking example of bureaucratic "resistance" was recently provided by Dr. Deborah Birx, the career bureaucrat who was selected to coordinate the Trump administration's coronavirus response. In 2022, Dr. Birx published *Silent Invasion: The Untold Story of the Trump Administration, Covid-19, and Preventing the Next Pandemic Before It's Too Late.*[15] She explains in the book that one duty of the response task force was to draft weekly reports with recommendations for state Covid-mitigation measures. Senior White House staff edited those recommendations before they were released. Dr. Birx writes that she disagreed with the edits, so she applied what she calls a "work-around" to White House review: she deleted every recommendation the White House rejected, but then reinserted the exact same recommendations in less prominent locations in the report.

Dr. Birx actually uses the terms "sleight of hand" and "subterfuge" to describe her method. In brief, the process was "write, submit, revise, hide, resubmit." She notes that her superiors "never seemed to catch this subterfuge." Despite her clear understanding that she was asked not to include certain provisions in these documents, she felt free to send out whatever she chose, as long as her superiors did not "catch" it. Dr. Birx's underhanded actions to advance her own policy views against those of democratically accountable officials—and without elevating her disagreement to a more senior official for resolution—are shameful and epitomize the failure of our current system. Even worse, her public boasting demonstrates just how divorced from our representative system of government the leaders of the civil service have become.

These examples should ring alarm bells for Americans, and a 2018 survey from Monmouth University shows that they have.[16] The study found that 60 percent of Americans believe that career federal employees have too much influence over policy. One key reason for career staff's outsized influence in policymaking—and for the difficulties faced by the political leadership in dealing with outright hostility—is the protections against removal gained by the civil service over time. These protections have resulted in an entrenched bureaucracy that frequently works for its own purposes and benefit.

But just as one bad apple doesn't ruin the whole bushel, there are still countless devoted, hardworking career civil servants in the federal government. After working as a copyist for three federal agencies (including the Department of the Interior), the great American poet Walt Whitman observed, "I found the clerks mainly earnest, mainly honest, anxious to do the right thing—very hard working, very attentive."[17] Public health experts, law enforcement officers, and other dedicated civil servants should be lauded for their service, just as bad actors should be held to account. Unfortunately, civil service protections coupled with ineffectual political leadership have weakened accountability to the point that many presidential appointees feel they have little ability to discipline or remove poor performers. As a result, unelected career civil servants have acquired unchecked discretion to advance their own policy preferences rather than those of the people's elected leaders. In the next chapters, we will examine how the absence of effective checks by either Congress or the judiciary has further empowered civil servants to wield their discretion with impunity.

CHAPTER THREE

UNELECTED RULE MAKERS

In 2012, the U.S. Fish and Wildlife Service (FWS) designated 9,577,969 acres as critical habitat for the northern spotted owl.[1] This is a massive geographic area, larger than the state of Maryland. That designation of critical habitat was challenged in federal court the following year. In 2015, the district court ruled that the plaintiffs who brought the litigation lacked standing, but this decision was reversed and remanded by the D.C. Circuit Court of Appeals. In 2020, the United States entered into a settlement agreement with the plaintiffs. As part of the settlement, the service agreed to consider engaging in a new rulemaking process regarding the northern spotted owl's critical habitat designation. Its proposed rule to modify the critical habitat was published in the Federal Register in August 2020, and the rulemaking process was concluding in the final days of the Trump administration.

The role that economic consequences and other related policy considerations should play in the designation of critical habitat is a longstanding point of contention. Under the Endangered Species Act of 1973, species are determined to be "endangered species" or "threatened species" without any consideration of economics. In early 1978, the Fish and Wildlife Service expressly rejected the idea of considering "socioeconomic or cultural factors unrelated to the biological needs of a listed species" in designating critical habitat.[2] Shortly after these regulations were issued, the Supreme Court decided *Tennessee Valley Authority v. Hill*, enjoining the completion of construction of the almost-finished Tellico Dam on the grounds that it threatened the snail darter with extinction.[3]

Congress quickly responded to what it viewed as overreach by the Supreme Court, amending the ESA with several changes to the law governing critical habitat. These amendments provided the secretary of the interior with the authority to factor economic considerations into exclusions from critical habitat designations in certain situations. Congress directed the secretary to evaluate effects on human activity before deciding whether to make a critical habitat designation. Congress also gave the secretary the authority to exclude an area from a critical habitat designation upon determining that the benefits of the exclusion outweigh the benefits of inclusion, *unless* the secretary determines that the exclusion will result in the extinction of the species. By making these amendments to the ESA, Congress provided the secretary with a means to minimize potential conflicts between human needs and the imperative of species conservation.

An illuminating discussion of this grant of authority—which initially was to apply only to invertebrates but was later broadened—was included in the House Merchant Marine and Fisheries Committee's report on the 1978 amendments. Previously, the determination of critical habitat had been "a purely biological question," whereas in the amended law, "[e]conomics and any other relevant impact shall be considered by the Secretary in setting the limits of critical habitat." The committee report continued:

> The result of the committee's proposed amendment would be increased flexibility on the part of the Secretary in determining

critical habitat for invertebrates. Factors of recognized or potential importance to human activities in an area will be considered by the Secretary in deciding whether or not all or part of that area should be included in the critical habitat of an invertebrate species. The committee expects that in some situations, the resultant critical habitat will be different from that which would have been established using solely biological criteria. In some situations, no critical habitat would be specified.[4]

In late 2020, the draft final critical habitat designation for the northern spotted owl that was the focus of the rulemaking would encompass approximately 6,105,279 acres.[5] This would be a substantial reduction from the 9,577,969 acres designated as critical habitat in 2012. Unsurprisingly, some were not happy about it. As the regulation was nearing finalization, I found myself reviewing a communication from an FWS employee who appeared to believe that he was free to replace the words of a statute with other words he wished that Congress had written instead. Besides presuming to have the authority to rewrite the law, the employee was critical of the contents of his agency's draft final rule.

In the employee's view, the scope of the exclusions could slow the owl's potential recovery and might lead to extinction at some point in the future. His conclusion rested largely on assumptions about federal land-use changes that might possibly happen if the lands in question were no longer designated as critical habitat. He appeared not to realize that the designation of critical habitat was not the only legal or policy consideration affecting federal land management policies and practices. To reach his conclusions as to the likely pace of change, he had to ignore a host of economic, legal, and political realities.

In addition, the employee seemed to think it meaningless that Congress, in delegating authority to the secretary of the interior to exclude an area from critical habitat designation, did so with only one clear statutory limitation: unless the exclusion "will result in extinction." The employee wished to replace the words that Congress wrote with "more likely than not" or "has a high likelihood to result in the extinction of the species," which he considered "more appropriate" in biological terms. While I appreciated his passion for the northern spotted owl, I was struck by his lack of regard for statutory language and by his reliance on conjecture about future land use. In my first tour of duty at Interior as the department's solicitor, I had issued a legal opinion on this particular statutory language, and that legal opinion had remained in effect through multiple administrations.

Examining the employee's communication along with a memorandum from the FWS director that laid out a contrary perspective, I was far from persuaded by the employee's concerns. Examining the facts and the law, I did not conclude that the exclusion of the areas in question from the previously designated critical habitat would result in the extinction of the northern spotted owl, for a variety of reasons.

First, whether the modification to critical habitat was made or not, federal land management agencies would be required to comply with their own legal obligations. For example, the ESA included a requirement that federal agencies avoid actions likely to jeopardize the continued existence of the northern spotted owl. Similarly, federal agencies and private parties would still be required to comply with Section 9 of the ESA, which strictly prohibits any "person," including any officer, employee, or agency of the United States, from "taking" any endangered or threatened fish or wildlife species, subject to criminal and civil penalties.[6] The ESA and its implementing regulations define "take" broadly to encompass killing, injuring, or harming listed species, including habitat modification or degradation that significantly impairs a species' essential behavioral patterns, such as spawning, rearing, migrating, and feeding.[7]

Congress provided only limited exceptions to this prohibition. Any assumptions regarding future activities on federal or private lands, and the consequences to the listed species, must acknowledge all these legal realities.

Similarly untethered from reality were the employee's speculations about the likelihood, pace, and magnitude of administrative and policy changes by other federal agencies that might affect the spotted owl's habitat at some point in the future. His assumptions about the likely pace of development rested on possible changes in administrative policy by the Bureau of Land Management and the Forest Service. This was a subject outside his expertise. It was in the realm of social and political science, an area in which I had some experience to draw upon in forming my own conclusions.

Moreover, the data suggested that the amount of designated critical habitat was not the most crucial factor in the fate of the northern spotted owl. Even with a massive land area already designated as critical habitat, plus millions of additional acres available to these owls in parks and wilderness areas, their estimated population had declined more than 70 percent since the listing of the species.[8] The stressor that currently has the largest negative effect on the species is the barred owl, which is invading the northern spotted owl's habitat and competing with it for resources. If anything is going to result in the demise of the northern spotted owl, it is far more likely to be the barred owl—absent an aggressive management regime—than a reduction of the area designated as critical habitat.

I penned a memorandum explaining my own conclusions and included it in the record. After I left the department, the employee's policy position won out under my successor, who decided to modify the final exclusion rule that was issued at the end of the Trump administration.[9] In my opinion, this action needlessly exacerbated conflict between people and wildlife, with scant evidence to suggest that it would improve the long-term condition of the northern spotted owl. The secretary's exercise of the exclusion authority is discretionary, however. More to the point, the Constitution authorized Congress—not the secretary of the interior, and certainly not a random employee at the Fish and Wildlife Service—to decide the scope of the secretary's authority.

Delegation of Lawmaking Authority

In many ways, our government today does not function by the consent of the governed as the Founders intended. For decades, much of the activity in the federal government has lacked accountability to the American people. Many government decisions of consequence to American citizens are made without a vote or much influence by elected members of Congress. Instead, the legislature typically delegates authority to administrative agencies to make decisions. Within these agencies, political appointees subdelegate many of their responsibilities to unelected career staff, often with little review or meaningful oversight, which further removes policy decisions from accountability to voters. The courts have permitted the delegation of lawmaking authority to agency officials based on the notion that the agency employees are ultimately accountable to the president. In theory, the president oversees the operations of the myriad departments and agencies of the executive branch. But the explosive growth of the administrative state and its workforce has increasingly strained presidential oversight.

As the complexity of government has increased, Congress has found it expedient to pass broad, vaguely written laws and rely on administrative agencies to fill in the gaps. Such laws often identify a general policy goal and then delegate power to executive agencies to achieve that goal through regulatory action based on expertise in a certain policy area. Congress in this way delegates authority to executive agencies to administer complex statutes and grants them the power to issue regulations with the force and effect of law.

At times, such broad grants of authority might violate the non-delegation doctrine—a principle of constitutional and administrative law holding that Congress cannot delegate its legislative powers to the executive or the judicial branch. In other words, lawmakers cannot allow other government actors or entities to make laws. Although the Supreme Court has not struck down a statute on nondelegation grounds in nearly a century, some legal scholars believe the doctrine serves as a limitation on the power of the administrative state because it seeks to ensure that policy decisions are made by politically accountable entities.[10] But as Justice Neil Gorsuch noted in 2022 in his concurrence in *National Federation of Independent Business v. Occupational Safety and Health Administration (OSHA)*, "Sometimes lawmakers may be tempted to delegate power to agencies to 'reduc[e] the degree to which they will be held accountable for unpopular actions.'"[11] Delegations of power to executive agencies allow members of Congress to shirk responsibility for unpopular policy decisions while leaving the American people with little recourse to hold the decision makers accountable.

The Supreme Court on Delegation

The United States Supreme Court has helped to delineate how much authority Congress can delegate to executive agencies because the Constitution vests the power to interpret the law in the judiciary. The court's reasoning over time has defined what qualifies as a permissible delegation of legislative authority to agencies and what is not permissible.

Wayman v. Southard (1825) is a landmark case in the nondelegation doctrine's development. The case concerned a delegation of authority from Congress to the federal courts allowing the courts to create their own judicial procedures. The court in *Wayman* held that such a delegation did not represent an unconstitutional delegation of legislative power. In the case opinion, Chief Justice John Marshall aimed to distinguish between Congress's legislative responsibilities and the subsequent rules and procedures necessary to implement legislative priorities. Marshall argued that while Congress should regulate its own legislative functions, any subordinate procedures that followed could be established by other entities. "The line has not been exactly drawn which separates those important subjects, which must be entirely regulated by the legislature itself, from those of less interest, in which a general provision may be made, and power given to those who are to act under such general provisions to fill up the details," he wrote.[12] The line-drawing problem first identified by Marshall has become a recurring theme in nondelegation doctrine cases.[13]

A century later, in *J. W. Hampton, Jr. & Co. v. United States* (1928), the Supreme Court sought to bring clarity to the line-drawing problem. The case involved legislation in which Congress delegated authority to the president to adjust tariff rates in order to protect American business. The legislation—a type known as contingent legislation—allowed the president to adjust tariff rates only if certain conditions were met. The court held that Congress had not delegated legislative power to the executive because the contingent legislation provided the president with clear instructions on when and how to adjust the tariff rates established by the law. In its reasoning, the court developed the "intelligible principle test" as a way to determine whether or not a congressional delegation of authority to the executive branch violates the nondelegation doctrine and the separation of powers, thus addressing Marshall's line-drawing problem. Writing for the court, Chief Justice William Howard Taft argued, "If Congress shall lay down by legislative act an intelligible principle to which the person or body authorized to fix such rates is directed to conform, such legislative action is not a forbidden delegation of legislative power."[14] The intelligible principle test provides some clarity on the degree of unique discretion that Congress may entrust to decision makers in the executive branch.

The Supreme Court went on to apply *J. W. Hampton*'s intelligible principle test in two 1935 cases: *Panama Refining Co. v. Ryan* and *A. L. A. Schechter Poultry Corp. v. United States*.[15] Both *Panama* and *Schechter* marked changes in the court's approach to the nondelegation doctrine and established a foundation for later decisions. The cases questioned whether separate provisions of the National Industrial Recovery Act (NIRA), a major component of President Franklin D. Roosevelt's New Deal, violated the nondelegation doctrine. Through the NIRA, Congress authorized the National Recovery Administration to seek input from both businesses and labor unions to replace existing antitrust laws with industry-wide "codes of fair competition." The Supreme Court in both cases found that the law made unconstitutional delegations of legislative authority. Applying the intelligible principle test, Chief Justice Charles E. Hughes argued that no such principle could be found in the relevant sections of the law. The lack of an intelligible principle to guide executive action, argued the court, allowed the president "to exercise an unfettered discretion to make whatever laws he thinks may be needed."[16]

The Supreme Court's rulings in *Panama* and *Schechter* effectively applied the nondelegation doctrine to gut the challenged provisions of the NIRA. The decisions shed light on the court's view of the appropriate limitation of congressional delegations of authority to the executive branch. The decisions also reemphasized the intelligible principle test as the court's primary tool for evaluating challenges to the delegation of authority. On this basis, the court went on to reject a number of nondelegation challenges, including *Mistretta v. United States* (1989), *Whitman v. American Trucking Associations, Inc.* (2001), and *Department of Transportation v. Association of American Railroads* (2015), among others.[17]

Though the Supreme Court has not invalidated a statute for violating the nondelegation doctrine since *Panama* and *Schechter* in 1935, statements by justices in *Gundy v. United States* (2019) indicated the potential for a revival of the doctrine. The court ruled 5-3 that

the challenged statute, the Sex Offender Registration and Notifica-
tion Act, did not violate the nondelegation doctrine, but dissenting
views from minority justices showed that a robust debate about the
doctrine was continuing among the members of the court.[18]

Justice Gorsuch discussed his approach to the nondelegation
doctrine in his concurrence in *National Federation of Independent
Business v. OSHA* in 2022.[19] This case challenged the Biden administration's Covid-19 vaccine mandate for certain private business
employees. Gorsuch argued that the mandate exceeded the authority that Congress delegated to the Occupational Safety and Health
Administration, describing the central question in the case as "who
decides?" Does an administrative agency in Washington have the
sweeping power to mandate vaccinations for private citizens? Or
does that power rest with the people's elected representatives in
Congress and local government?

Gorsuch's reasoning centered on the "major questions doctrine,"
a concept that is related to the nondelegation doctrine and would
be formally adopted by the court later that year in *West Virginia v.
Environmental Protection Agency*. This doctrine requires Congress to
put forth clear directions when it tasks an agency to regulate issues
that have great economic and political consequence. "The major
questions doctrine is closely related to what is sometimes called
the nondelegation doctrine," wrote Gorsuch. "Both are designed
to protect the separation of powers and ensure that any new laws
governing the lives of Americans are subject to the robust democratic
processes the Constitution demands." OSHA issued its vaccine mandate through statutory authority allowing the agency to promulgate
emergency regulations to address harmful exposure to substances in
the workplace. But Gorsuch found that the agency had overstepped
its authority. Previous use of that authority had concerned narrow
workplace issues such as exposure to asbestos or other toxic substances. OSHA's Covid-19 vaccine mandate, according to Gorsuch,

sought to broaden the agency's purview to "regulate not just what happens inside the workplace but induce individuals to undertake a medical procedure that affects their lives outside the workplace."

Gorsuch's concurrence highlighted a key question of political accountability that the nondelegation doctrine and the major questions doctrine both seek to address: Who decides? The power to make significant decisions affecting individuals' private conduct rests with the people's elected representatives, not with unelected agency staff. By applying these doctrines, Gorsuch explained, the judicial branch can help guard "against unintentional, oblique, or otherwise unlikely delegations of the legislative power."

How Delegation Expands Agency Power

Around the time of the *Panama* and *Schechter* decisions, President Franklin D. Roosevelt found himself faced with a problem: a burgeoning bureaucracy with a variety of approaches to administration. In 1936, he formed a presidential committee to study administrative processes in executive agencies. The President's Committee on Administrative Management (also known as the Brownlow Committee, being chaired by Louis D. Brownlow) issued a report criticizing what the committee viewed as an absence of coordination among agencies and a lack of oversight by the president. The report found that the executive branch "is badly organized; that the managerial agencies are weak and out of date; that the public service does not include its share of men and women of outstanding capacity and character; and that the fiscal and auditing systems are inadequate."[20]

The findings of the Brownlow Committee contributed to Roosevelt's establishment of the Attorney General's Committee on Administrative Procedure in 1939. This committee issued nearly five hundred pages of recommendations in 1941, laying the foundation for the first version of the federal Administrative Procedure Act (APA), which was passed in 1946. The APA established uniform procedures for federal agencies, including rulemaking procedures for agencies to follow in exercising their delegated authority from Congress to issue binding regulations.

The APA established two rulemaking processes for agencies: formal rulemaking and informal rulemaking, also known as notice-and-comment rulemaking. The two processes have similar requirements for the publication of proposed and final rules in the Federal Register. Proposed rules must include the proposed effective date and the legal authority under which the agency is proposing the rule, as well as the substance of the rule. In both rulemaking processes, agencies are required to solicit public feedback on the proposal and to publish a revised final rule in the Federal Register at least thirty days before it is scheduled to take effect. The public feedback step is different between the two procedures, however. In the formal rulemaking process, agencies must conduct a hearing on the record with procedures similar to those used in a court of law, usually overseen by an administrative law judge who serves as an impartial adjudicator. These proceedings are burdensome. Informal rulemaking—the process that agencies use for the vast majority of rulemaking—takes a less structured approach to gathering public input. It generally requires agencies to provide a period of time for interested parties or any members of the public to submit written comments and recommendations on a proposed rule.

Agency use of formal rulemaking procedures has dramatically declined since the Supreme Court decided *United States v. Florida East Coast Railway* in 1973.[21] This decision held that formal rulemaking is required only when a governing statute calls for a hearing "on the record." The subsequent growth in informal rulemaking led Justice Clarence Thomas to describe formal rulemaking as the "Yeti of administrative law" in his 2015 concurrence in *Perez v. Mortgage Bankers Association*.[22] The informal rulemaking process is a faster way for agencies to implement a president's policy agenda in a narrow window of time, but critics note that it decreases transparency and accountability by moving away from the formal procedures that call for hearings on the record and the cross-examination of experts.

The unchecked delegation of decision-making authority allows unelected agency employees to promulgate rules that constitute significant policy decisions, often with little political oversight. The public can't remove agency employees from their positions if they make unpopular policy decisions, but elected lawmakers *can* delegate authority to agencies and thus evade responsibility for any of the negative consequences or costs that may result from subsequent agency rulemaking.

Joseph Postell, an administrative law scholar, illustrated the tension between delegation and political accountability in his 2016 article "'The People Surrender Nothing': Social Compact Theory, Republicanism, and the Modern Administrative State." Postell traced the nondelegation doctrine's roots to social compact theory, which suggests that society developed from a voluntary agreement between individuals to live and protect their rights together. Postell likened social compact theory to a principal-agent relationship between the people and their elected representatives. The people are the principal that has delegated lawmaking ability to the legislature. But unlike other principal-agent relationships—such as that between a private employer and an employee—the people have no opportunity to authorize any further delegations of legislative power to the executive branch. According to Postell, such delegations go against social compact theory, which holds that "only the people can delegate legislative power, and when legislative power is delegated by the people to their agents in the legislature, the legislature cannot delegate its powers away because legislative power was never fully alienated by the people."[23]

Some Consequences of Delegation in Executive Agencies

When there is no meaningful political accountability surrounding agency exercise of delegated authority, career staff may be motivated to use the rulemaking process to advance their own policy interests. Agency staff who disagree with a policy put forth by an elected political leader can slow-walk or derail a rulemaking effort by producing work of such poor quality as to be unusable. During the Trump administration, for example, leadership in the U.S. Department of Agriculture (USDA) encountered resistance when they attempted to repeal the Roadless Rule, implemented in 2000 under the Clinton administration. The Roadless Rule was perceived by many, including state political figures, as inappropriately designating millions of acres of land administered by the U.S. Forest Service (an agency within the USDA) as off-limits to development. The resulting lack of a road system on large swathes of federal land hindered mining and logging activity that was legal in those areas. As a consequence, all but two of the logging mills in Alaska were shut down, which was perceived as badly hurting the economy in the southeastern region of the state. The Bush administration tried to repeal the rule but failed, largely due to procedural errors.

After learning how the Roadless Rule was viewed in Alaska, President Trump suggested the repeal of its application to that state. The original nationwide rule, as described by James Sherk, had been produced in less than a year by career staff at the Forest Service, an agency led by a career official rather than a political appointee. Repealing the rule in just one state was a much smaller task, yet these career staff delivered unusable material—despite their prior experience going through the process of withdrawing the rule under the Bush administration.[24] The staff disagreed with President Trump's policy, so they gummed up the machinery. What should have been an expeditious process took over two years and required heavy editing and rewriting by political appointees.

Delegated authority also poses problems when overzealous agency staff take positions that are inconsistent with established agency precedent. I had been the deputy secretary at the Department of the Interior for only a couple of weeks when I became aware of what is now a public example of overzealous staff at the Fish and Wildlife Service. While I was on a trip to Montana in August 2017, Secretary Zinke's office asked me to set up a last-minute meeting with someone who had a longstanding issue with the service's interpretation of the Endangered Species Act. The individual was represented by counsel, so I suggested that he have his counsel provide me with the relevant materials he wanted the agency to review. Soon I learned of a dispute between the Los Angeles District of the U.S. Army Corps of Engineers and the Arizona Ecological Services Office of the FWS.

The dispute was basic. Essentially, the two federal agencies had different views on the appropriate application of Section 7 of the ESA to a proposed real estate development project in Southern Arizona. Section 7 requires federal agencies to consult with the FWS to ensure that their actions, such as the issuance of permits, are not likely to jeopardize the continued existence of a federally listed species or to destroy or adversely modify the listed species' designated critical habitat. The Army Corps of Engineers issues Clean Water Act permits for dredging or filling in the nation's navigable waters. The developer in Arizona sought a permit from the corps because of the possibility of filling washes (dry stream beds that occasionally channel water), and in 2006, after consulting with the FWS, the corps issued a permit authorizing the discharge of fill material to fifty-one acres of "waters" with the proposed residential development.

The financial crisis put the real estate project on ice. In 2016, a new developer acquired it and decided to move forward with a modified plan. Meanwhile, portions of off-site parcels of land that would be used for wetlands mitigation had been proposed for inclusion in critical habitat for the northern Mexican garter snake and the yellow-billed cuckoo, though no listed species were found within the area of the proposed development itself. Understanding that the developer could go ahead and build the modified project without getting a new permit, the Corps of Engineers sought to consult with the FWS only on impacts related to the off-site mitigation parcels rather than the entire development. The field supervisor for the Arizona Ecological Services Field Office, on the other hand, took the position that the whole project should be included in the review. The two agencies disagreed on the proper scope of the Section 7 evaluation, in part because the Arizona field supervisor's opinion diverged from the FWS's own regulations and handbooks. Another reason was disagreement on whether the developer would actually be willing to move forward without a new permit from the Corps of Engineers.

Communication between the developer and the Department of the Interior, however, made clear that the residential development plan would proceed without the permit if necessary, albeit in a modified fashion that wouldn't affect navigable waters. Rather than filling washes, for example, the developer would build around them. In other words, the developer would either construct Plan A (the original project) *with* the permit, or build Plan B, which did not require a permit. The rules of the FWS state that, in certain situations, if a potential impact to a listed species (in this case, the consequences of the construction and the activities associated with a residential development) would occur whether or not an agency action took place (in this case, whether or not the Corps of Engineers issued a Clean Water Act permit to the developer), the effects of such impacts are not attributable to the agency's action for the purposes of Section 7 evaluation. Since the developer was going to move forward in constructing the residential development with or without a permit, any impacts resulting from that development were not attributable to the action of the corps. Thus, the evaluation of potential impacts from the decision to issue a new permit was limited to consequences on the off-site mitigation parcels.

From my quick review of the material, it appeared likely that the supervisor's position was inconsistent with the FWS's own existing consultation handbook (developed in the 1990s and upon which the public relied), and inconsistent with precedent from the Ninth Circuit Court of Appeals.[25] In my role as deputy secretary, I was authorized to exercise the secretary's authority to "supervise all public business relating to the Service."[26] This included making an effort to determine the legality of approaches taken by the Arizona field supervisor and other employees in the agency. So I headed to the department's lawyers to ask them to look into the dispute and provide their opinion to the FWS.

Interior's top Section 7 expert in the Office of the Solicitor reviewed the issue and counseled the Arizona office that "there is no 'but for' causal link between the Army Corps of Engineers' action and the proposed real estate development," since the developer had stated his intention to move forward with a modified version of the development without a permit if necessary. Over time, the corps and the real estate developer provided additional clarity on the facts of the proposed project, which further supported the expert attorney's opinion. The Arizona field supervisor subsequently, in 2017, concurred with the determination of the U.S. Army Corps of Engineers.

Given my understanding of the facts and the clear legal guidance, I assumed that everyone involved had reached the same conclusion as to the facts and the law. After all, to the extent that the Arizona field supervisor disagreed with the legal advice provided by the Section 7 expert attorney, he could have elevated the issue to management, either in the FWS or in the Office of the Solicitor, for higher-level review. The employee did neither. Instead, he brought his decision into conformity with the law and the facts. As he crafted his new decision, the employee wrote that while he did not believe his prior decision was "wrong at the time," FWS could now "confidently say there was no longer but for causation." He even explained his new decision to the press and continued to communicate with the media after their stories ran, affirming his rationale for the revised decision.

Nevertheless, the field officer later cried "Political interference!" After retiring, he claimed that political appointees in the department had "rolled" or "pressured" him into revising his decision and said he felt that his "authority was usurped." Yet he had developed and executed the action in writing himself. Moreover, he seemed not to understand that the authority he exercised had been delegated to him, starting from the secretary of the interior, down through the deputy secretary, the assistant secretary for fish and wildlife and parks, the director of the Fish and Wildlife Service—each of them a principal officer of the United States, nominated by the president and confirmed by the Senate—and on down the thread of delegation until it got to him. Those delegations of authority all included a requirement to follow the FWS's regulations, regardless of his personal views. His postemployment comments triggered a series of news articles, resulting in another review by the Arizona Ecological Services Office in May 2019, which reaffirmed the decision made in 2017 to withdraw the objection to the permit.

Overreach by zealous agency staff can have even larger consequences in these polarized times. Following the news stories about the field officer's claims of being "pressured," Representative Raul Grijalva (D) of Arizona, a vocal opponent of the proposed real estate development project, initiated an oversight investigation through his role as chair of the House Natural Resources Committee. The Department of the Interior's subsequent document submission to

Congress contained a clear statement on the appropriateness of the 2017 decision. But in February 2021, the Biden administration added fuel to the fire by initiating its own review of that decision. Four months later, the same official who in 2019 had reaffirmed the FWS's 2017 decision withdrew it. In July 2021, the Army Corps of Engineers too reversed course, suspending its permit and withdrawing its 2017 decision letter. In May 2022, after failing to interview the lawyer who provided the legal guidance to the FWS and without including Interior's written response to Congress, Rep. Grijalva and Rep. Katie Porter (D), chair of the House Natural Resources Subcommittee on Oversight and Investigations, sent a letter to Attorney General Merrick Garland seeking a criminal investigation, alleging a connection between the legal counsel, the Arizona office, and political donations. While their letter to Garland lacked a reasonable basis and nothing came of it, this episode demonstrates just how complex a single action can become when agency staff unilaterally exercise their delegated authority to take an unreasonable agency position that does not square with the law, the regulations, or the agency's own guidance. Their overzealous actions can affect regulated parties and government operations long after they are gone from their positions.

Some government employees apparently think their actions are not bounded by the words of a regulation or a law, particularly when a situation does not easily fit within the agency's current regulations. In the fall of 2017, shortly after entering the Department of the Interior as deputy secretary, I witnessed that kind of attitude as I reviewed draft biological opinions examining the consequences to listed species from the registration of malathion as a pesticide by the Environmental Protection Agency (EPA). The Fish and Wildlife Service uses specific regulations to evaluate the effects on listed species in Section 7 consultations.[27] These regulations contain very specific definitions that were developed in the Reagan administration.

Several specific definitions together create a regulatory paradigm in which agency employees tasked with drafting a biological opinion should: 1) identify an area called an "action area"; 2) figure out what is happening to listed species in that area in the absence of the federal agency's proposed action (in this case, the registration of a pesticide); and 3) compare the likely future of the species with and without that action occurring. This requires looking at several different types of effects to a listed species that are defined in FWS regulations and have been interpreted in particular ways for decades. These regulations define the "action area" to mean "all areas to be affected directly or indirectly" by the agency's action.[28] In this case, the FWS needed to identify the area of the "direct" and "indirect" effects to the listed species caused by the EPA's potential approval of a pesticide registration.

I read a draft biological opinion from the FWS that had been under development for years, and it appeared to rely on an understanding of the agency's regulations that was completely inconsistent with longstanding regulatory definitions of relevant terms. In developing their draft biological opinion, the service appeared to have relied on a National Academy of Sciences report from 2013 that addressed the issue. The EPA and the FWS, along with a few other agencies, had asked the academy to help them develop a consensus approach on how to access risks to listed species. Federal agency lawyers explained to the academy the longstanding regulatory text defining "indirect effects" under the ESA. "Indirect effects" are defined as "those that are caused by the proposed action and are later in time, but still are reasonably certain to occur,"[29] Which is a high threshold. But the academy explicitly rejected this view, saying that the agency lawyers' longstanding interpretation "could be quite restrictive and is quite different from most ecologists' understanding of indirect effects."[30] While the agency lawyers were bound by the regulatory text, the academy's scientists felt free to ignore it. The FWS staff then thought they could simply follow those scientists' suggestion and adopt "most ecologists' understanding of indirect effects," disregarding the language of their own binding regulations and nearly fifty years of their agency's interpretation of that language.

This interpretation of "indirect effects" was of great consequence for the EPA's proposed pesticide registration. To demonstrate an indirect effect under the regulations, the FWS record needed to show that the consequences for the species it predicted from the EPA's action were actually indirect effects *as defined by the regulations*, irrespective of the academy's view. Given the manner in which pesticides are manufactured, transported, and distributed, it was unlikely that there would be any consequence to a listed species from the EPA's registration until the application of the pesticide by some party at some point in the future. Establishing that effects "caused by EPA's action" were "reasonably certain to occur" at some later time would require a high degree of assurance as to where and when a particular pesticide was going to be applied. But there was virtually no data to support a reasonable certainty that the specific pesticide would be applied in any particular area.

I brought Interior's lawyers along with FWS employees into my conference room and asked for an explanation of how the approach taken in the draft opinion was consistent with the regulations. The service's employees could not provide an answer. The lawyers demurred, saying that they had just recently been given the draft document to review. I told them to review it and come back to explain how my understanding was in error. They concluded that my understanding was spot on. The draft was fatally flawed in the context of the written regulations. In my view, the FWS had wasted years of effort, not just by their employees but also by members of the public who had engaged in a multiyear process to develop this biological opinion.

Subsequently, a Democratic senator called for an inspector general investigation of my involvement in reviewing this document. The IG's report explained that the "attorneys said that after they reviewed the draft biological opinion on malathion they agreed with Bernhardt's observations, and that he raised valid legal concerns."[31] The disconnect between agency lawyers and staff in trying to solve complex problems leads to federal decisions that are unlikely to survive judicial review. It also undermines public confidence that agency employees are actually applying the law rather than implementing their personal preferences through regulatory action.

This incident highlights a common problem with regulatory action: the regulations developed by agency employees and lawyers are applied from the perspective of ecologists or other specialists in the field who may have given little thought to the actual words of the regulations. They might focus on the desired policy outcome of a particular decision rather than its legality, and the result is arbitrary and lawless action. It is true that regulations written by lawyers don't always translate well in the field, but regulatory definitions, whatever their flaws, are binding upon agency specialists unless they move to change the regulation. The public relies on the words in the regulations to understand what the rules are, so agency employees must adhere to those words. In the case of the pesticide registration, the Fish and Wildlife Service didn't want to make the effort to get the rules changed, so instead they essentially decided to ignore the regulatory limitations and proposed to apply what they wanted the rules to be. Such an approach was unlikely to be legally defensible.

Just as agency lawyers may write regulations that aren't well suited to the situation on the ground, agency specialists are sometimes asked to write regulations where they have no understanding of the underlying law. The matter of determining whether the polar bear was either a threatened species or an endangered species—as mentioned in the introduction—was an extremely high-profile listing proposal, largely because the listing petition had asserted climate change as the primary threat to the polar bear.

At the time, listing the polar bear was thought to be potentially the first such decision made by the government in connection with climate change. One might think the drafters of the rule would therefore have taken great care in putting together an experienced team to develop the proposed and final regulation, but that was not the case. In the Fish and Wildlife Service, the process of drafting a rule is assigned to local field offices, and the assignment to develop the polar bear regulation was sent to an office in Alaska, where staff tasked an employee to write the rule.

A year later, I received the draft final rule submitted to D.C. headquarters by the Alaska office, and it was not worth the paper it was printed on. First, the staff member assigned to draft the rule, while an expert in marine mammals, had never before written a regulation determining that any species was either an endangered species or a threatened species. I couldn't believe it. This rulemaking was viewed by the public as the biggest, most controversial listing by the FWS in eons, and who wrote the rule? A polar bear expert who had no prior experience with the application of the ESA. The law and the facts work together, and the employee charged with drafting the rule had little knowledge of the relevant law, however strong his command of polar bear facts may have been.

One thing the polar bear expert did understand about the law was that in order to determine whether a species is a threatened species under the ESA, you have to look into the foreseeable future and assess whether the species is likely to become endangered. If this is not likely, you can't list the species as threatened. The polar bear expert decided that the foreseeable future in this case was forty-five years, which is roughly three generations of polar bears.

When I read the draft final rule, I asked myself, what in the world does three generations of polar bears have to do with the foreseeable future? Foreseeability, according to the law, is what you can predict to the point that it's not speculative. That is how a lawyer understands foreseeability. From the perspective of the polar bear expert, however, biologists typically need studies covering at least three generations of a species to assess population dynamics and then make projections into the future on that basis. The "frequently asked questions" section of the proposed rule provided this reasoning:

> The ESA does not define "foreseeable future." In other ESA listings, it has often been interpreted to be a function of generations of the species in question and/or habitat regeneration cycles. In this status review, based on the opinion of polar bear experts, the Service has adopted three generations as the upper limit. Using this measure, since a polar bear generation is defined as 15 years, the "foreseeable future" addresses the next 45 years.[32]

In short, the FWS took an interval of time normally used in seeing trends looking backward, and declared the same interval to be the "foreseeable future." This was not at all consistent with the law. Because those tasked with writing the draft final rule had little understanding or appreciation of the law, department staff had to launch an all-hands-on-deck operation to rewrite the rule. It needed to align more closely with the requirements of the ESA if it was to have any chance of being successfully defended. The final rule defined the foreseeable future "in terms of the timeframe over which the best available scientific data allow us to reliably assess the effects of threats on the polar bear."[33] This definition tied the secretary's projection of the future to the available data rather than an arbitrary timeframe.

Policymaking by Guidance Document

Another way that policy can be influenced is through guidance documents. These are issued by political appointees, and sometimes by career employees, to inform employees of the agency's policy position, to interpret laws and regulations for interested parties, or simply to change the agency's practices. Guidance documents come in many forms, including memoranda, notices, interpretive rules, policy statements, bulletins, directives, news releases, letters, and even blog posts. Since they are not required to go through the APA's notice-and-comment process, guidance documents are technically not legally binding, but they might have that effect in practice. This reality can lead to questions of whether the guidance should have been subjected to the APA's notice-and-comment procedures. Political appointees or agency staff may at times suggest issuing guidance in lieu of doing the hard work of completing a rule, even when they know this practice is legally questionable.

In 1992, the Administrative Conference of the United States (ACUS) described how the use of binding guidance could infringe on the rights of regulated parties. As ACUS officials explained, "It may be difficult or impossible for affected persons to challenge the [guidance] within the agency's own decisional process," either to challenge its lawfulness or to question its wisdom. Affected persons could seek administrative remedies or judicial review of an agency's enforcement actions after the fact, but that is a long and costly process, which might well end in judicial deference to the agency. As a practical matter, "affected parties have neither the opportunity to participate in the process of policy development nor a realistic opportunity to challenge the policy when applied within the agency or on judicial review."[34]

Professor William Funk, in 2011, echoed these concerns about the use of agency guidance documents. He and ten other legal scholars agreed that agencies should be able to issue such documents, but worried about the abuse of that ability:

> [We all agree] that agencies must be able to issue certain interpretations and policy statements, generically guidances, without having to follow the notice-and-comment process applicable to legislative rules. On the other hand, everyone also agrees that agencies can abuse the ability to avoid notice and comment rulemaking through the invocation of the exceptions for "interpretative rules" and "general statements of policy." How to police the line between those rules requiring notice and comment and those that do not is what has stymied courts and commentators.[35]

In 2019, President Trump attempted to address this problem through Executive Order 13891, which aimed to prohibit federal agencies from issuing binding rules through guidance.[36] Several agencies, including the Department of Labor and the Department of Justice, then issued rules to implement the order. These rules created searchable databases of all agency guidance documents, required agencies to issue significant guidance documents (generally those with an economic impact of $100 million or more) through the informal rulemaking procedures, and allowed members of the public to petition agencies to amend or withdraw guidance documents, among other provisions. Despite the gains in guidance document transparency brought about by EO 13891, President Joe Biden repealed the order shortly after taking office, and agencies rolled back their transparency initiatives.

The Biden administration has also encouraged agency staff to take action on climate according to their own principles rather than calling on Congress to pass a law for that purpose. In late 2021, the Bureau of Land Management conducted fifteen listening sessions where agency staff could share their thoughts about how the agency might address climate change. A report on the listening sessions stated that the more than 3,200 comments gathered from the process "may be used to help inform and influence new policies and business practices to allow the BLM to tackle the climate crisis."[37] Instead of asking Congress for the authority to regulate climate-related issues, the political appointees asked the agency's career employees to brainstorm actions they would like to take, irrespective of the agency's authority or funding.

"A Particular and Recurring Problem"

On the final day of the Supreme Court's 2022 term, Chief Justice John Roberts issued a majority opinion in *West Virginia v. Environmental Protection Agency* holding that the EPA could not singlehandedly remake the U.S. energy sector through regulation without clear authorization from Congress. This was the first Supreme Court decision to invoke the "major questions doctrine." The court explained that this moniker "took hold because it refers to an identifiable body of law that has developed over a series of significant cases all addressing a particular and recurring problem: agencies asserting highly consequential power beyond what Congress could reasonably be understood to have granted." Like other jurists and scholars, the justices "recognized the common threads between those decisions."[38] The court's explicit embrace of the doctrine signals a potential for returning power to the American people instead of a bureaucracy in Washington, D.C.

West Virginia v. EPA arose from one of President Barack Obama's attempts to bypass Congress. In his first term, Obama tried to get Congress to pass a cap-and-trade law to reduce carbon emissions. He candidly admitted that "under my plan of a cap-and-trade system, electricity rates would necessarily skyrocket." Unsurprisingly, supersizing energy bills was unpopular with voters and their elected representatives. Thus, despite large Democratic majorities in both houses of Congress, the Senate never even voted on the bill. President Obama then ordered the bureaucracy to gin up new regulations to reduce carbon emissions. The resulting Clean Power Plan (CPP) was a big deal. The Obama administration estimated it was equivalent to taking more than two-thirds of U.S. passenger vehicles off the road. Cap-and-trade couldn't get through Congress, but the EPA, with some legal gymnastics, decided it could impose a version of cap-and-trade on its own. The administration wanted to fundamentally reshape the energy market while avoiding the need to secure the approval of Congress.

Unfortunately, the federal government often operates this way. When I ran the Department of the Interior, I directed career attorneys to list all the department's statutory duties explicitly dealing with "climate change." There were only two: helping the Department of Energy with a report, and writing another report on water issues. Nonetheless, leftist members of Congress would frequently call on the department to "stop climate change!" Instead of working to build a consensus in Congress to pass a law, they wanted Interior to transform America by itself. I would tell these members of Congress to pass their law and then I would faithfully execute it. The Obama administration's EPA was not so restrained.

During the Trump administration, the EPA replaced the Clean Power Plan with the Affordable Clean Energy (ACE) plan, based on the traditional understanding of the Clean Air Act. In February 2021, a liberal panel of the D.C. Circuit Court of Appeals struck down the ACE rule and held that the EPA could impose cap-and-trade type policies.

The Supreme Court rejected the D.C. court's arguments in its *West Virginia* decision, concluding that "it is not plausible that Congress gave EPA the authority to adopt on its own such a regulatory scheme.... A decision of such magnitude and consequence rests with

Congress itself, or an agency acting pursuant to a clear delegation from that representative body."[39] In other words, creatively reinterpreting the law to discover sweeping grants of previously unknown authority doesn't cut it.

There are three big takeaways from this decision in the short term. First, the federal agencies would be wise to be judicious in their assertion of what the court described as "highly consequential power beyond what Congress could reasonably be understood to have been granted," but don't hold your breath on this happening. Second, the various federal district courts and federal courts of appeals will have to determine how they apply this doctrine, and the Supreme Court may well have to weigh in a few times before we see the real magnitude of the ruling. Third, Congress should recognize that it would behoove them to strive for more clarity in their grants of authority to agencies. The bottom line, however, is that if the federal judiciary pays homage to the *West Virginia* decision, it will likely mean that the people make the rules through their elected representatives—not federal bureaucrats. Agency officials do not stand for election. They have no democratic mandate to impose sweeping societal changes unilaterally. The court's application of the major questions doctrine has the potential to protect individuals and businesses from agencies that act without political accountability.

The principle that authority rests with the people's elected representatives in Congress is basic, and unsurprisingly the American people agree with the Supreme Court. Polling conducted by Scott Rasmussen near the time of the *West Virginia v. EPA* decision showed that Americans by a margin of 42 percent to 31 percent trust voters and their elected representatives more than government agencies and policy experts to formulate major regulations. A plurality of Americans also believe that the EPA should need approval from Congress before issuing regulations to limit greenhouse gasses. The court's decision could signal the return of governing authority to the American people.

The concentration of power in administrative agencies has effectively shifted the exercise of lawmaking power from the people's elected representatives to unelected agency staff. The public can't hold agency employees accountable for their actions by voting them out. Lawmakers, for their part, often prefer to duck responsibility for negative consequences by punting difficult policy decisions to administrative agencies. Without effective accountability, agency career staff can leverage their delegated authority and the rulemaking process to run roughshod over the policy preferences of elected political leaders and the will of the American people. This shifting of power gives rise to an antidemocratic scenario in which the public can't hold the government accountable at the ballot box. In the next chapter, we'll examine how career staff can take advantage of agency enforcement practices as another means to advance their own preferences.

CHAPTER FOUR

THE ENFORCERS

The 116th Congress (January 3, 2019 to January 3, 2021) passed 344 new bills into law. Over the same period, federal administrative agencies finalized more than 6,300 new regulations. Federal agencies also issued an unknown number of guidance documents that established policies with little or no transparency for regulated parties. It's impossible for individuals to stay informed of the countless new legal requirements churned out by administrative agencies that affect their daily lives, and yet it's imperative. A citizen who runs afoul of an administrative agency may face great peril.

We have seen how the administrative bureaucracy can act as an unaccountable, unelected fourth branch of government, and how broad congressional delegations of authority combined with the lack of meaningful political accountability can result in agency regulations that are unresponsive to the public will. In this chapter, we'll examine how agencies are tasked with enforcing the rules they make and adjudicating any resulting disputes. Agency enforcement and adjudication proceedings, while well intentioned, can compound the problem of the lack of political accountability. Agency adjudicators, for example, have the potential to decide cases in the best interest of their employing agency (at the expense of citizens), often without practical oversight by political appointees. Their decisions can drive agency policy without going through the public notice-and-comment requirements of the rulemaking process. Selective enforcement of agency policies by career enforcement staff, moreover, can create different systems of justice depending on whether the activities in question are in line with the prevailing worldview in the agency. One result is a crisis in confidence of due process protections for American citizens who find themselves in violation of agency rules.

Adjudication

When an agency brings an enforcement action against an individual for violating an agency rule, the dispute is usually resolved through an in-house process known as adjudication. The phrase "agency adjudication" is generally understood to mean an agency action with the force of law that resolves a claim or dispute between parties in a particular case. Parties may be drawn into adjudication for a number of reasons. The agency may have found that an individual violated one of the laws it enforces. The individual, on the other hand, may have appealed an agency action, such as the denial of public benefits or of a license or permit. The agency resolves the dispute through an adjudication process ending in an agency order.[1]

Trial procedure in the United States traditionally follows an adversarial model: opposing parties dispute claims and present evidence in court before a mostly passive referee (the judge) and the finder of fact (judge or jury).[2] Congress adopted this adversarial model from the judiciary for formal federal agency adjudication in 1946 by enacting the Administrative Procedure Act (APA).[3] Formal adjudications work in a manner similar to a court trial and feature minimum standards of due process protections for citizens, such as the opportunity to cross-examine agency experts. Formal adjudication must be presided over by an administrative law judge (ALJ), acting as an impartial adjudicator. However, the APA also provides for informal adjudication, which can take a variety of forms according to the agency-specific statutes. Informal adjudication generally operates with less rigid formality. Agency adjudicators known as administrative judges (AJs) often preside over informal adjudication, but this is not necessarily the case.

The Adjudicators

Neither the administrative law judges (ALJs) nor the administrative judges (AJs) who serve as agency adjudicators are "judges" in the traditional sense, as they are not members of the independent Article III judiciary. They have the authority to hold hearings, review findings, and administer rulings, but normally they are only exercising authority delegated from the department secretary or from the leader of their employing agency.

Provisions of the APA are intended to ensure that ALJs—those who preside over formal adjudication—maintain a degree of independence from their employing agency. For example, ALJ's may not perform (or report to employees who perform) investigative or prosecutorial duties. Agencies cannot subject ALJs to performance reviews or award them bonuses, nor can they discipline or fire ALJs except for "good cause" as determined by the Merit Systems Protection Board (MSPB). The competitive recruitment and examination process for ALJs, formerly administered by the U.S. Office of Personnel Management (OPM), was intended to provide another safeguard against agency influence. Agencies could hire ALJs only from a list of candidates vetted by the OPM (though this precedent has changed in recent years, as we will see). A number of federal agencies employ their own ALJs, including the Department of the Interior, the Social Security Administration, the Department of

Labor, the Department of Agriculture, and the Drug Enforcement Administration.[4]

The nature of ALJ independence is occasionally questioned. Are they really as independent as they claim? The *New York Times* and the *Wall Street Journal* have both reported on the win rate of the Securities and Exchange Commission (SEC) in its in-house adjudication proceedings. The *Times* found that the SEC had an 88 percent success rate in its 2011 adjudication proceedings, as against a 63 percent success rate in Article III courts on appeal.[5] The *Journal* found that the SEC won in 90 percent of its adjudication proceedings between late 2010 and early 2015, compared with 69 percent of its cases on appeal to Article III courts.[6] Lillian McEwen, an SEC ALJ from 1995 to 2007, told the *Journal* that she received criticism from the agency's chief ALJ for finding in favor of defendants too often. McEwen also claimed that ALJs "were expected to work on the assumption that 'the burden was on the people who were accused to show that they didn't do what the agency said they did,'" thus shifting the burden of proof from the accuser to the accused, in violation of due process.

The question of ALJ independence was at the forefront of a 2018 ruling by the Supreme Court in *Lucia v. Securities and Exchange Commission (SEC)*, which changed the appointment process for ALJs.[7] The justices found that the ALJs at the SEC were "Officers of the United States" who must be appointed by the president, the courts, or agency heads under the Constitution's appointments clause—not by agency staff. In response to the ruling, President Trump issued Executive Order 13843, which removed ALJs from the competitive civil service and reclassified them as members of the excepted service.[8] This change was intended to give agencies the ability to consider specialized agency and legal expertise when filling ALJ positions, rather than requiring them to select from one of the top three generalist candidates vetted by the OPM. It also removed a potential constitutional conflict between the prior process and the appointments clause.[9]

While *Lucia* determined that ALJs will generally be considered officers under the appointments clause, other recent cases have raised constitutional questions about ALJs' statutory protections against removal (that is, they can be removed only for cause). Lawmakers provided for such removal protections in the APA in an effort to safeguard ALJ independence from the employing agencies. As a result, ALJs had enjoyed *multilevel* removal protections. They could be removed only for cause, and that cause was determined through an adjudicatory process by the Merit Systems Protection Board, whose members themselves could be removed only for cause. In the 2010 case *Free Enterprise Fund v. Public Company Accounting Oversight Board*, the Supreme Court held that Congress could not give multiple levels of good cause removal protections to officers of the United States. The court held that these protections go too far in insulating such officers from presidential oversight, thus limiting the president's ability to carry out his constitutional duty to "take care that the laws be faithfully executed."[10]

In a recent case out of the United States Court of Appeals for the Fifth Circuit, *Jarkesy v. Securities and Exchange Commission* (2022), a three-judge panel held that the SEC ALJs' multilevel removal protections are unconstitutional. "SEC ALJs perform substantial executive functions," wrote Judge Jennifer Walker Elrod in the opinion. "The President therefore must have sufficient control over the performance of their functions, and, by implication, he must be able to choose who holds the positions. Two layers of for-cause protection impede that control; Supreme Court precedent forbids such impediment."[11] The future of ALJs' multilevel removal protections appears dim as courts continue to weigh in on the appropriate scope of ALJ independence. A case pending before the Supreme Court, *Cochran v. Securities and*

Exchange Commission, questions whether individuals subjected to SEC enforcement proceedings can concurrently challenge the constitutionality of the action in an Article III court, or if they have to wait until the ALJ issues a final order in their SEC enforcement proceedings before they can do so.

By comparison with ALJs, administrative judges (AJs) enjoy fewer statutory protections to safeguard their impartiality and their independence from the employing agencies. AJs are hired directly by the agency, can be disciplined or fired by agency staff, and are subject to performance reviews and financial incentives. (According to research by Professor Kent Barnett in 2016, some AJs even perform other duties for their employing agencies when not hearing cases.)[12] AJs now far outnumber ALJs, because agency use of formal adjudication has declined in favor of informal adjudication. According to the American Bar Association, informal adjudication makes up nearly 90 percent of agency adjudication proceedings.[13] As a consequence, federal agencies in 2017 employed not quite two thousand ALJs but more than ten thousand AJs and other non-ALJ adjudicators (such as hearing officers, immigration judges, and other informal adjudicators). This means that challenges to agency decisions are much likelier to be adjudicated by people with relatively limited independence from the agency leadership.

How Adjudication Shapes Agency Policy

Whether through formal or informal procedures, ALJs and AJs make decisions that can serve to set agency policy outside the rulemaking process. The Administrative Conference of the United States (ACUS), in fact, found in 2013 that some agencies set policy more often through adjudication than by rulemaking.[14] At times, adjudication can proceed with little political oversight, so career agency adjudicators may have leeway to advance their own policy objectives. In addition, agency adjudication can raise questions about due process shortcomings related to transparency and fair notice.

The Supreme Court has allowed for policymaking through adjudication since 1947 with its decision in *Securities and Exchange Commission (SEC) v. Chenery Corp.*, a case also known as *Chenery II*.[15] The court held that whether to enact a policy through rulemaking or adjudication was up to the agency's discretion. Writing for the majority, Justice Frank Murphy argued that agency adjudication orders are the "product of administrative experience, appreciation of the complexities of the problem, realization of the statutory policies, and responsible treatment of the uncontested facts. It is the type of judgment which administrative agencies are best equipped to make and which justifies the use of the administrative process." He concluded, "Whether we agree or disagree with the result reached, it is an allowable judgment which we cannot disturb." Murphy claimed that the need for flexibility sometimes requires agencies to lean more heavily on adjudication than on rulemaking.[16]

Legal scholars nonetheless have long raised concerns about agencies setting policy through adjudication. In 1980, for example, William Mayton argued in the *Duke Law Journal* that Congress created the rulemaking process with public accessibility in mind.[17] Setting agency policy through adjudication, according to Mayton, doesn't live up to the transparency and due process standards of the rulemaking procedure, such as giving fair notice. Kent Barnett observed that policymaking through adjudication rather than rulemaking is also problematic from a political leadership perspective because the vast majority of agency adjudicators (ALJs and AJs) have protections against removal that insulate them from direct presidential control.[18] The preferred policies of administrative adjudicators may not always align with those of the people's elected president. To address this issue, some departments, such as Interior, crafted policies making clear that the solicitor's legal opinion is binding on those adjudicators. In other departments, insulated actors may still have the power to issue orders that drive agency policy with little political oversight or accountability, particularly if the good-cause removal protections stand.

Enforcement

Just as agency adjudicators can leverage the adjudication process to set agency policy, enforcement staff can drive agency policy through selective enforcement of rules. Like adjudication, administrative enforcement often operates with little direct oversight by political appointees, which allows career staff the latitude to stymie cases they personally disagree with. As described in Chapter 2 through the work of James Sherk, career staff in the Civil Rights Division at the Department of Justice ducked cases when they disagreed with the administration's interpretation of the law. Staff would slow-walk cases they didn't agree with and would fail to communicate with political appointees.

One example of this practice involved a discrimination complaint brought against Yale University in 2020. After years of stalling and foot-dragging by career staff, a Department of Justice investigation found that Yale heavily discriminated against white and Asian applicants for admission. The Educational Opportunities Section of the DOJ Civil Rights Division, which litigates cases of racial discrimination in education, should have handled the dispute, but none of the staff were willing to work on the case. Political appointees drafted the complaint against Yale themselves, and to pursue the litigation they needed to pull together a team of career staff from less ideological DOJ offices, primarily the Civil Division and the U.S. Attorney's Office for Connecticut. Through deliberate inaction—simply failing to enforce the federal law—staff at the DOJ attempted to influence the department's approach to racial discrimination in admission practices.

High-profile cases like the one against Yale caught the attention of political appointees, but many others that ran counter to the staff's policy preferences may have fallen by the wayside. There are 350 career lawyers and fewer than twenty political appointees in the Civil Rights Division, which makes close oversight challenging. Political appointees may be highly dependent on the professionalism and ethics of the career attorneys to carry out the president's agenda consistent with the law.

Selective enforcement by executive agencies caused headaches for a group of beachfront communities in New Jersey during my tenure as secretary of the interior. Representative Jeff Van Drew (then a Democrat) approached me about a proposed beach replenishment project that the Fish and Wildlife Service was opposing, which would likely impose significant unnecessary costs on those communities. The issue centered on the Coastal Barrier Resources Act (CBRA), which generally prevents nonemergency development on areas designated as coastal barriers. It was intended to reduce wasteful federal spending and protect our natural resources. An exception in the law allows federal funding for sand removal from system areas to remedy beachfront erosion outside the designated barrier areas in certain circumstances, such as to stabilize existing shorelines or to protect sensitive environmental areas. The New Jersey communities had carried out three nonemergency beach replenishment projects since 1996, creating over a mile of critical habitat for migratory birds, and the FWS had not raised any objections.

In 2016, however, the local field office abruptly challenged the proposed beach replenishment, claiming it did not satisfy the legal exception. The objection was based on a longstanding but flawed interpretation of the CBRA that apparently had been ignored in New Jersey between 1996 and 2016. Now the agency wanted to prohibit the same kind of project it had previously accepted. The result would be a skyrocketing cost to the communities for continuing to stabilize their shoreline.

After meeting with Representative Van Drew and community leaders in 2019, I reviewed the language of the CBRA and its legislative history. I found that the basis of the objection made by FWS career staff in 2016 and in the legal memorandum purporting to provide support for it was flawed. The Office of the Solicitor issued a directive clarifying that the CBRA included an exception allowing those New Jersey communities to move sand from within the barrier system to stabilize their shorelines and protect vulnerable wildlife.

The FWS's application of a flawed interpretation of the CBRA gave the agency more power while placing unneeded costs and burdens on those communities—which is exactly what Congress was trying to avoid when it created the statutory exemption. The mayor of Avalon, Martin Pagliughi, summed up the situation in the local *Cape May County Herald*: "Some individuals at the Service ignored language in a federal law and put coastal communities at unnecessary risk despite agreement from federal, state, municipal and environmental interests that they were dead wrong in their position. We simply will not get rolled by individuals with specific agendas and will continue to make best decisions based on science, and not egos."[19] A clear interpretation of the law helped these towns for a short time. Unfortunately, the Biden administration reverted back to the flawed reading of the CBRA, asserting that the statute was ambiguous, and once again subjected certain coastal communities to needless burdens that Congress had tried to prevent.

Due Process and Agency Enforcement Actions

The Fifth Amendment of the Constitution states that the federal government cannot deprive a person "of life, liberty, or property, without due process of law." The Fourteenth Amendment extended this requirement to the state governments, declaring, "nor shall any State deprive any person of life, liberty, or property, without due process of law."

There are two kinds of due process: procedural and substantive. *Procedural* due process, in the context of administrative law, refers to protections for citizens against arbitrary actions by government agencies that threaten to deprive them of life, liberty, or property. It is specific to the legal procedures that administrative agencies are required to follow in rulemaking and adjudication proceedings. *Substantive* due process, on the other hand, involves the application of administrative law as it relates to individual life, liberty, or property interests.

The APA outlines specific procedural due process protections for citizens engaging with the administrative state. These protections are designed to prevent administrative agencies from violating individual rights. But the increasing use of informal adjudication—making the trial-like, on-the-record hearing required by formal adjudication nearly obsolete—arguably poses challenges for procedural due process. Some scholars claim that the flexibility of informal adjudication allows agencies to develop procedures that suit their case volume and needs. Paul Verkuil, former chair of ACUS, viewed the shift toward informal adjudication as a move that provided agencies with more decisional freedom under the due process clause:

> From its earlier position in *Wong Yang Sung* of equating due process to formal APA hearings, the Court has evolved from the *Goldberg* requirement of specifying procedures for due process to a world that can readily accept an informal process of infinite variety. In this environment the decider need not be APA-qualified, nor must the APA formal hearing process serve as a baseline. This informal process, which is not defined by the APA, remains an amorphous competing model.[20]

Other scholars, however, view the shift to a more flexible approach as detrimental to due process. Philip Hamburger raised several concerns about this trend in *Is Administrative Law Unlawful?*(2016). He argued that closed adjudication proceedings unconstitutionally prevent members of the public from coming to the defense of individuals whose rights are violated. The Sixth Amendment provides criminal defendants with the right to a public trial, while the First Amendment provides the public and the press with the right to access court proceedings. But administrative adjudication subverts these requirements, according to Hamburger.

> In private administrative chambers, the public cannot monitor what agencies do and cannot come to the defense of defendants who are denied their rights. Defendants cannot even observe how similarly situated defendants are treated. As a consequence, in administrative hearings, "a man may lose his cause or receive great prejudice...for want of defense."[21]

Defendants in agency proceedings, moreover, do not have an explicit right to counsel.[22] They may choose to obtain legal representation, but if they cannot or do not, the lack of legal defense raises additional concerns about the ability of individuals to secure their rights in the face of agency action.

Due process is further challenged when agencies charge individuals with criminal penalties, thus muddying the waters between agency adjudication and criminal cases in Article III courts. In the last month of its 2021 term, the Supreme Court decided a double jeopardy case that bore on issues with federal agency adjudication, specifically in the Department of the Interior's Court of Indian Offenses. A dissent from Justice Neil Gorsuch joined by Justices Sonia Sotomayor and Elena Kagan appeared to tee up a significant question of due process for future cases related to that court, with broader implications as well.

Denezpi v. United States centered on a member of the Navajo tribe who was prosecuted and convicted in federal court soon after pleading guilty in connection with the same actions in the Court of Indian Offenses. The Supreme Court majority ruled that the double jeopardy clause had not been violated since a different "offence" was charged in each case. In his dissent, Gorsuch argued that this reasoning was flawed because the same prosecuting authority—the United States government—was charging the same defendant twice for the same act.[23] Pointing to the due process clauses, Justice Gorsuch noted that the Constitution does not allow successive prosecutions by one sovereign based on another sovereign's laws.[24] The dissent raised further concerns about a situation that allows "federal bureaucrats to define an offense; prosecute, judge, and punish an individual for it; and then transfer the case to the resident U.S. Attorney for a second trial for the same offense under federal statutory law."[25]

It is likely that few people have ever heard of the Court of Indian Offenses. It originated in 1882 when the secretary of the interior, H. M. Teller, wrote to his department's Office of Indian Affairs (now known as the Bureau of Indian Affairs) to suggest that the office "formulate certain rules for the government of the Indians on the reservations." Subsequently, the commissioner of Indian affairs adopted regulations prohibiting certain acts and directing that a "Court of Indian Offenses" be established for nearly every Indian tribe or group of tribes to adjudicate rule violations.[26] Five of these courts currently serve sixteen of the more than five hundred federally recognized Native American tribes. Other tribes have their own tribal courts, which they operate pursuant to their inherent sovereign authority, while the Court of Indian Offenses is "part of the Federal Government."[27] For Mr. Denezpi, this meant that federal agency officials "played every meaningful role in his case: legislator, prosecutor, judge, and jailor."[28]

Certainly, the Department of the Interior's role here as "legislator, prosecutor, judge, and jailor" is extraordinary. The department regulations list crimes created by federal agency officials.[29] These include tribal crimes, to the extent that the tribal ordinances are "approved by the Assistant Secretary [of] Indian Affairs or his or her designee."[30] That assistant secretary appoints the court magistrates subject to a confirmation vote by the governing body of the tribe that the court serves. However, the assistant secretary retains full authority to "appoint a magistrate without the need for confirmation by the Tribal governing body."[31] The assistant secretary may remove magistrates for cause of his own accord or upon the recommendation of the tribal governing body.[32] Unless a contract with a tribe provides otherwise, a department official appoints the prosecutor for each court.[33]

The dissenting justices in *Denezpi* observed that "governments generally may not deprive citizens of liberty or property unless they do so according to 'those settled usages and modes of proceeding' existing at common law."[34] Time will tell whether agency adjudicatory procedures comply with the constitutional protections of due process, but Justices Gorsuch, Sotomayor, and Kagan seem skeptical.

Agency adjudication in cases that carry criminal penalties violates citizens' right to a trial by jury in criminal cases, argues Philip Hamburger. He and others also argue that the absence of juries in administrative adjudication (where the adjudicator acts as both judge and jury) violates the Seventh Amendment by denying due process to individuals who are subject to criminal penalties. Hamburger contends that later access to a jury on appeal in an Article III court doesn't remedy the original lack of due process in agency adjudication, and the problem is compounded when cases on appeal lack a jury altogether.

A three-judge panel of the United States Court of Appeals for the Fifth Circuit signaled support for Hamburger's due process claims in the *Jarkesy* decision. "The Seventh Amendment guarantees Petitioners a jury trial because the SEC's enforcement action is akin to traditional actions at law to which the jury-trial right attaches," wrote Judge Jennifer Walker Elrod. "And Congress, or an agency acting pursuant to congressional authorization, cannot assign the adjudication of such claims to an agency because such claims do not concern public rights alone."[35]

Another due process challenge arises when agencies threaten individuals with monetary penalties that are out of proportion with the alleged violation.[36] For example, in 2014 the Environmental Protection Agency threatened a Wyoming farmer, Andy Johnson, with up to $20 million in fines for constructing a livestock pond on his property. The agency claimed that the pond was in violation of the Clean Water Act, despite an explicit exemption for stock ponds in the law and the fact that the pond did not actually affect any navigable waters. The penalty would have resulted in Johnson's financial ruin. In an effort to avoid litigation, Johnson and the agency reached a settlement in 2016. Since the agency had clearly overstepped the law, Johnson did not have to pay any penalties and he could keep the pond on his property. He merely agreed to enhance the environmental benefits that the pond itself would provide, and the EPA in turn dropped all enforcement of the case.[37]

Andy Johnson was able to avoid financial devastation, but not all defendants are so lucky. The threat of exorbitant monetary penalties, regardless of whether or not the violation was intentional, can lead individuals to walk on eggshells lest they be slapped with a hefty agency fine.

Mike and Chantell Sackett faced the threat of excessive monetary penalties when they broke ground on the construction of their dream home in a residential subdivision in northern Idaho. The EPA quickly ordered them to halt construction. Seven months later, after countless requests by the Sacketts for an explanation, the EPA finally provided the rationale for its decision. The agency claimed that the Sacketts' lot constituted a "navigable water" subject to regulation under the Clean Water Act, even though it had no water source. The EPA threatened the Sacketts with exorbitant civil fines upwards of $75,000 a day and potential criminal penalties unless they abandoned their plans and restored the land. As if that weren't severe enough, the EPA denied the Sacketts an avenue to contest the reasoning behind its determination. With no other recourse available, the Sacketts finally sued the EPA in an Article III court. The case went all the way to the Supreme Court, where the justices unanimously held that the Sacketts had the right to challenge the EPA's claim of jurisdiction over their land in an Article III court.[38] After twelve years of court proceedings, when the case was pending before the United States Court of Appeals for the Ninth Circuit in 2020, the EPA withdrew its compliance order and moved to dismiss the case as moot, which was rejected. Then the Ninth Circuit upheld a lower court's determination that the EPA had jurisdiction over the Sacketts' property.[39] But the Sacketts have continued to pursue the agency in courts to gain clarification on whether the EPA has jurisdiction over their property in the first place. As of this writing, their case is once again pending before the Supreme Court.

These cases and others like them raise questions about the extent of due process protections available to individuals who are subject to agency enforcement. President Donald Trump issued two executive orders aimed at shoring up procedural due process protections. In 2019, he issued Executive Order 13892, which sought to curb what the order referred to as administrative abuses by requiring agencies to provide the public with fair notice of regulations. The next year, he issued a Regulatory Bill of Rights in Executive Order 13924, which put forth a set of fairness principles in administrative enforcement and adjudication, and directed agencies to comply with the principles where appropriate as part of their response to the coronavirus pandemic. The order emphasizes general principles of promptness, fairness, and transparency in adjudication and enforcement proceedings, as well as more specific procedural due process protections such as requiring that adjudication be free from governmental coercion and that agency adjudicators be independent of enforcement staff.[40]

President Joe Biden rescinded both of Trump's procedural due process executive orders shortly after taking office, vaguely arguing that the orders hindered the federal government's ability to deal with the coronavirus pandemic, economic recovery, racial justice, and climate change.

This chapter touched on a few of the major due process concerns in agency adjudication, but there are many others that Congress has failed to remedy. In the absence of meaningful political accountability, agency staff have a tremendous amount of room to push the enforcement envelope. I believe we might be far better off if every enforcement action against a private party required the express authorization of a principal officer of the United States who was subject to Senate confirmation. As we will see in the next chapter, those who manage to navigate the enforcement process and appeal agency adjudicative orders to independent Article III courts may face another hurdle of the administrative state: the practice of judicial deference.

CHAPTER FIVE

ABSENT JUDGES
AND A WEAK CONGRESS

B etween 2001 and 2005, I served as Interior's point person for the development of legislation that would eventually become the Energy Policy Act of 2005. I first worked on the establishment of the National Energy Policy Development Group and then led the department's efforts to work with members of Congress on enacting provisions associated with Interior that were part of the policy development group's plan. In August 2005, once the law was enacted, I led the coordination of implementing those provisions.

One of the key provisions of the bipartisan Energy Policy Act was Section 322, which clarified that a type of natural gas drilling known as hydraulic fracturing, or fracking, was excluded from federal regulation. A historical legal precedent had previously viewed the Environmental Protection Agency as having authority to regulate fracking under the Clean Water Act, but Section 322 clearly stated that fracking was not to be regulated at the federal level. Instead, the various states were charged with fracking oversight within their borders. It was curious, then, to watch the Department of the Interior under the Obama administration attempt to regulate an activity that Congress had clearly excluded from the EPA's purview and implicitly from the federal regulatory paradigm in general. Despite this legislative action, Interior aggressively tried to stretch its regulatory authority to include fracking, with the claim that Congress had granted the department broad delegations of authority over oil and gas development and the management of public lands generally, and that this allowed it to regulate fracking. But the federal judiciary would push back against this claim.

The State of Wyoming challenged a rule to regulate fracking issued by the department's Bureau of Land Management in 2015. The bureau claimed that several statutes delegated to it the authority to regulate fracking, chiefly the Mineral Leasing Act of 1920 (MLA) and the Federal Land Policy and Management Act of 1976 (FLPMA). The MLA granted the BLM broad authority to issue regulations to carry out the law, which generally aimed to promote oil and gas development on public lands. The FLPMA similarly authorized the bureau to manage renewable and nonrenewable public land resources to meet the needs of current and future generations. Since those statutes were vaguely formulated and broad in scope, the district court in Wyoming might have chosen to follow the precedent of deferring to an agency's own view of its delegated authority under the law. But Section 322 of the Energy Policy Act tipped the scales, and the court declined to accept Interior's effort to stretch its authority like a rubber band beyond the intent of Congress.

In *State of Wyoming v. Department of the Interior*, decided in June 2016, the district court found that, while the laws cited did grant broad regulatory authority to the BLM, no law specifically gave the agency the authority to regulate fracking. Moreover, Section 322 of the Energy Policy Act explicitly removed fracking from the EPA's regulatory purview. Congress had clearly spoken on the issue in that law, yet the BLM tried arguing that this limitation did not pertain to them. As far as the court was concerned, however, if Congress had stripped the EPA of regulatory authority over fracking, it had also stripped all federal agencies of any such authority. "Having explicitly removed the only source of specific federal agency authority over fracking," wrote Judge Scott W. Skavdahl in the opinion, "it defies common sense for the BLM to argue that Congress intended to allow it to regulate the same activity under a general statute that says nothing about hydraulic fracturing."[1]

Under the Trump administration in 2017, the Department of the Interior formally withdrew the Obama-era rule in response to an executive order aimed at eliminating needless barriers to energy production. Unsurprisingly, the withdrawal of the rule was challenged by special interest groups. A court ruling in 2020 finally upheld the decision to withdraw the regulation.[2]

The Wyoming court's reasoning illuminates how the anticipation of judicial deference to agency interpretations of law encourages aggressive action by the executive branch, even in the face of explicit limitations by Congress. Judges have crafted deference doctrines in the name of respecting the subject-matter expertise of agency officials in complex cases, but these doctrines also incentivize the zealous search for ambiguities that might justify a stretching of agency authority, since the agencies recognize that the judicial branch will be a very limited check on that effort. Courts are thus ceding much of their constitutional authority to interpret the law to the executive branch, while lax political oversight allows this power to be wielded by largely unaccountable career staff in administrative agencies. This chapter takes a close look at the transfer of judicial power to the executive branch through the development and application of deference doctrines. It also discusses how courts can help reverse the trend.

Judicial Review

If individuals subject to agency adjudication receive a decision that they believe is in error, they can normally appeal the decision through the agency's internal appeals process. When that avenue is exhausted, the agency's adjudication decision becomes a final agency action.[3] The Administrative Procedure Act (APA) allows individuals who feel they have been wronged by a final agency action to appeal for judicial review by an Article III court.

The Supreme Court first explicitly recognized the right to judicial review of an adverse agency decision in the 1902 case *American School of Magnetic Healing v. McAnnulty*. The court held that an individual on the receiving end of a harmful agency decision has the right to seek judicial review of the agency's order by an Article III court when the agency has acted beyond the scope of its statutory authority.[4] Judicial review of agency actions helps guard against abuses of power. The courts can serve as a check on agencies that exceed the bounds of their statutory authority. Edward Re, an administrative law scholar, praised judicial review of agency actions in 1991, writing that it "is a tribute to the American legal system that any person can challenge governmental action in a court of law, and have the realistic expectation that, if there is a legitimate relevance, the wrong or grievance will be redressed."[5]

The APA allows for Article III judges to review agency actions that are "arbitrary, capricious, or an abuse of discretion." It doesn't allow for judicial review of final agency actions in all instances, such as when Congress explicitly prevents judicial review of certain grievances, or when the agency action in question is "committed to agency discretion by law." Since the APA's exceptions are explicit and narrow, the courts generally presume that agency actions are subject to judicial review. The Supreme Court emphasized this presumption in the 1967 case *Abbott Laboratories v. Gardner*, calling for an examination of congressional intent before a court declines judicial review. The court stated that "only upon a showing of 'clear and convincing evidence' of a contrary legislative intent should courts restrict access to judicial review."[6]

Judicial Deference

When a challenge to agency action comes before an Article III court, the common assumption is that independent, neutral judges will review the agency's action and determine whether or not it was lawful. In practice, however, judges often defer to agency interpretations of statutes without independently interpreting the law. This effectively tilts the playing field in favor of the federal executive branch.

Judicial deference is a principle of judicial review in which a federal court accepts an agency's interpretation of either an ambiguous statute that Congress directed the agency to administer or an ambiguous regulation issued by the agency itself, even if the judges would have arrived at a different conclusion as to the meaning of that language. At times, courts conclude that an agency's legal interpretation of a statute or a regulation is the best interpretation of the language, and when that happens there is no need to apply the principle of deference to resolve a legal question. For example, a panel of the United States Court of Appeals for the District of Columbia Circuit arrived at such a conclusion in *Guedes v. Bureau of Alcohol, Tobacco, Firearms, and Explosives* (2022), finding that "there is no need to decide what deference, if any, a regulation should receive where we can conclude that the agency's interpretation of the statute is the best one."[7] When such an alignment between judicial and agency interpretations doesn't occur, judges often defer to an agency's statutory or regulatory interpretation. As a result, the Supreme Court over time has developed a number of deference doctrines to guide judges in reviewing agency actions. Deference doctrines can essentially compel judges to accept agency positions and prevent the judiciary from overruling an agency's reasonable interpretation of an unclear law.

Supporters of this practice claim that deference respects the specialized knowledge of neutral agency experts and prevents courts from imposing statutory interpretations developed by judges who lack subject-matter expertise. President Franklin Roosevelt's advisor James Landis viewed Article III judges as "jacks-of-all-trades and masters of none," with "breadth of jurisdiction and freedom of disposition."[8] Landis and his contemporaries believed that such judges should not weigh in on the determinations of neutral experts in complex policy matters.

Courts most often rely on three primary deference doctrines in administrative law: *Chevron* deference, *Skidmore* deference, and *Auer* deference. The first of these doctrines stems from the Supreme Court's 1984 ruling in *Chevron v. Natural Resources Defense Council*, which requires a federal court to yield to an agency's reasonable interpretation of an ambiguous statute that Congress instructed the agency to carry out. In other words, if Congress passes a law that requires an agency to take a particular action but isn't explicitly clear about how the agency should take that action, *Chevron* deference holds that the courts will accept an agency's reasonable interpretation of what Congress intended. Justice Antonin Scalia succinctly described the doctrine as "the principle that the courts will accept an agency's reasonable interpretation of the ambiguous terms of a statute that the agency administers."[9]

Courts follow a two-step process to apply *Chevron* deference. First, judges must determine if Congress expressed clear intent in the statute to guide agency action on the question at issue. If the statute is clear, then agencies must follow congressional intent. If the statute is unclear, then the *Chevron* inquiry proceeds to the second step, in which courts evaluate the reasonableness of the agency's statutory interpretation. If a court finds the interpretation to be reasonable, the *Chevron* doctrine prevents the judges from substituting their own interpretation of the statute if they would have arrived at a different conclusion about its intended meaning. This mechanism is designed to support the notion that agency actors are responsible for carrying out the law and have more subject-matter expertise than judges do.

Since the development of *Chevron*, the Supreme Court has adopted additional deference doctrines to guide judicial review of agency actions. Unlike *Chevron* deference, these doctrines don't necessarily require a court to defer to an agency's position, but they may suggest such a path. Two often-cited forms of deference, *Skidmore* deference and *Auer* deference, are both based on Supreme Court decisions issued in the 1940s, though they didn't coalesce into formal doctrines until after *Chevron* was decided in 1984. According to Justice John Paul Stevens's opinion in *Chevron*, while no formal deference doctrines were in place at the time, the court had "long recognized that considerable weight should be accorded to an executive department's construction of a statutory scheme it is entrusted to administer."[10] Justice Scalia echoed this claim in a lecture at Duke Law School in 1989, saying that "courts have been content to accept 'reasonable' executive interpretations of law for some time."[11]

Skidmore deference derives its name from the 1944 Supreme Court decision in *Skidmore v. Swift & Co.* In his opinion in that case, Justice Robert H. Jackson wrote:

> We consider that the rulings, interpretations, and opinions of the Administrator under this Act, while not controlling upon the courts by reason of their authority, do constitute a body of experience and informed judgment to which courts and litigants may properly resort for guidance. The weight of such a judgment in a particular case will depend upon the thoroughness evident in its

consideration, the validity of its reasoning, its consistency with earlier and later pronouncements, and all those factors which give it power to persuade, if lacking power to control.[12]

This reasoning is behind what later became known as *Skidmore* deference, which was formally developed as a doctrine with the court's decision in *Christensen v. Harris County* in 2000. Unlike *Chevron* deference, *Skidmore* deference does not compel judges to defer to an agency's interpretation of a statute. Instead, it allows the court to be persuaded by the agency's ability to demonstrate that its interpretation is based on valid reasoning. In the *Christensen v. Harris County* opinion, Justice Clarence Thomas highlighted another key distinction between *Chevron* and *Skidmore* deference: while *Chevron* deference is binding for agency rules developed through administrative rulemaking, *Skidmore* deference is normally applied to agency interpretations issued through guidance, "such as those in opinion letters—like interpretations contained in policy statements, agency manuals, and enforcement guidelines."[13]

While *Chevron* deference and *Skidmore* deference give judges direction when they interpret statutes, *Auer* deference provides direction when they are tasked with interpreting agency regulations. *Auer* deference is named for the 1997 Supreme Court decision in *Auer v. Robbins*. It is also known as *Seminole Rock* deference because the *Auer* decision reaffirmed a deference approach first described in the court's 1945 ruling in *Bowles v. Seminole Rock & Sand Co.* Justice Frank Murphy's opinion in that earlier case reasoned that a court must yield to an agency's interpretation of its own unclear regulation unless the court finds that the interpretation is "plainly erroneous or inconsistent with the regulation."[14] Later formalized in *Auer*, this doctrine holds that a federal court must defer to an agency's reasonable interpretation of an ambiguous regulation that the agency has issued.

The 2019 case *Kisor v. Wilkie* narrowed the scope of *Auer* deference. Justice Elena Kagan delivered the opinion of the court, which upheld the concept of *Auer* deference while putting forth new limits on its application:

- *Auer* deference applies only when the regulation in question is actually ambiguous.
- *Auer* deference applies only if the regulation in question is an authoritative or official agency position.
- Agency expertise determines whether *Auer* deference applies in certain circumstances. *Auer* deference is less appropriate for questions that fall outside an agency's regular duties.
- In order for *Auer* deference to apply, the reasonable agency interpretation of an ambiguous regulation must not create unfair surprise for regulated parties.

In a concurring opinion, Justice Neil Gorsuch argued that the majority opinion limited *Auer* deference in such a way that the doctrine emerged "maimed and enfeebled—in truth, zombified."[15] He favored eliminating the doctrine altogether, saying that even the weaker version of *Auer* deference could impose unnecessary legal hurdles on litigants and deny independent judicial decisions. Justice Brett Kavanaugh agreed in a separate concurring opinion, also arguing that the traditional tools of statutory interpretation should provide enough clarity for judges to avoid deferring to agencies.

The Transfer of Judicial Power to Agencies

When courts accept agency interpretations of statutes, they arguably cede their constitutional authority to determine what the law is. Executive agencies rather than courts, in this dynamic, possess the power to interpret the law. In 1989, Justice Scalia described judicial deference to agency interpretations as an abdication of judicial duty:

> I suppose it is harmless enough to speak about "giving deference to the views of the Executive" concerning the meaning of a statute, just as we speak of "giving deference to the views of the Congress" concerning the constitutionality of particular legislation—the mealy-mouthed word "deference" not necessarily meaning anything more than considering those views with attentiveness and profound respect, before we reject them. But to say that those views, if at least reasonable, will ever be binding—that is, seemingly, a striking abdication of judicial responsibility.[16]

Deference facilitates the expansion of agency power by restricting the judiciary's exercise of its constitutional duty to interpret the law, shifting much of that responsibility to unelected agency actors. Broad interpretations of the law can allow agencies to stretch their regulatory purview over Americans' everyday lives in ways that Congress never contemplated. When judges cannot or do not check their activity, executive agencies are encouraged to push the limits of their authority further and further from what Congress intended.

Another concern about deference is that it contravenes the nondelegation doctrine, which states that Congress cannot delegate lawmaking authority to executive agencies. Professor Cynthia Farina suggested that the concept of judicial deference in itself violates the nondelegation doctrine by anticipating congressional delegations of policymaking power to agencies through ambiguous laws.[17] Justice Gorsuch observed that nondelegation doctrine concerns stemming from judicial deference are compounded by the notion that agencies can change their interpretations of statutes over time, leaving no consistent standard to guide regulated parties.[18] The dual abdications of lawmaking and judicial responsibilities through delegation and deference have thus contributed to the power of executive agencies and the growth of the administrative state.

The Future of Judicial Deference

Since the first articulation of the *Chevron* deference doctrine, it has been cited in legal arguments tens of thousands of times. Kenneth Starr, former solicitor general under President George H. W. Bush, even praised the doctrine as a Magna Carta for use in federal administrative agency deregulation during the Reagan administration.[19] Justice Antonin Scalia and Justice Clarence Thomas initially expressed support for the doctrine after its development. As we have seen, Scalia soon became critical, and recent clues from other justices suggest that judicial attitudes toward deference could be turning more skeptical.

Chevron deference in particular is seen by some to be "entering a period of uncertainty, after long seeming to enjoy consensus support on the Court," according to Professor Michael Kagan. He noted that all nine justices on the court in 2018 had "at least once signed an opinion explicitly holding that *Chevron* should not apply in a situation where the administrative law textbooks would previously have said that it must apply." Since 2015, Kagan observed, an environment has emerged "in which it seems that the Court may be more willing to explicitly refine the doctrine, to limit its application in certain ways, and to articulate new exceptions."[20]

Deference has fallen out of favor with members of the Supreme Court as well. Justice Thomas, for instance, has reversed his early support of deference, writing in the 2015 case *Michigan v. Environmental Protection Agency* that his changed views on deference "derided his own prior majority opinion."[21] Chief Justice John Roberts, in his concurring opinion in *Kisor*, intriguingly stated that the court's decision upholding *Auer* deference did not translate into support for *Chevron* deference.[22] Justice Kavanaugh, in his separate *Kisor* concurring opinion, agreed with the chief justice, as well as echoing Justice Gorsuch's call to eliminate *Auer* deference altogether.[23]

Inconsistent applications of deference doctrines have also raised concerns among judicial observers. Michael Kagan noted that uncertainty about the consistent application of *Chevron* had circulated since the doctrine's inception.[24]

Some observers optimistically see the Supreme Court's embrace of the major questions doctrine in *West Virginia v. Environmental Protection Agency* as a limitation on *Chevron*'s effects, even though the court did not overturn *Chevron*. For example, shortly after *West Virginia* was decided, David B. Rivkin Jr. and Mark Wendell DeLaquil opined, "Absent a clear statutory delegation of the power to regulate, the executive branch can't regulate at all. Where statutory language is clear enough to grant regulatory authority, it should eliminate substantial ambiguity about how that authority can be exercised." In their view, *West Virginia* "effectively strips agencies of much of their regulatory willfulness, compelling them to regulate only as Congress intended. The domain of Chevron deference is limited to filling in the interstitial details of statutes in which Congress has decided the policy stakes." From this point forward, Rivkin and DeLaquil asserted, "the first question in any important case concerning agency power is whether Congress actually intended for the agency to be regulating at all, not whether agency attorneys were clever enough to find a vague statute to justify the new rule."[25] If the courts take this approach, *West Virginia* could be a major step toward reining in administrative agencies and restoring political accountability.

Sue and Settle

Various laws include provisions that allow citizens or interested groups to sue the agency that administers the law when the agency fails to carry out a statutory requirement, such as meeting a regulatory deadline. The agency may choose to settle the litigation rather than take it to court. The settlement agreement may require the agency to issue a rule on a particular subject or within a certain timeline. It may also specify conditions of the rule, such as the entities that will be covered. Agency officials can settle litigation in a way that restricts the decisions of future policymakers by requiring specific procedural and policy outcomes as part of a judicially enforceable settlement.

In my experience, entering a consent decree or settlement agreement can be a prudent use of taxpayer resources, avoiding costly, drawn-out litigation that an agency is likely to lose. Many policymakers and legal scholars, however, have expressed concern that such litigation has given rise to a practice known as "sue and settle," in which interest groups weaponize litigation to undermine the procedural safeguards of the rulemaking process established by Congress, and to cut the public out of agency decision making.

Supporters of sue and settle argue that settlements force agencies to act in the face of illegal inaction, such as when agency staff fail to meet a legal obligation that is reviewable. A settlement agreement commits the agency to compliance. Courtney McVean, an attorney, and Justin R. Pidot, a law professor, made this argument in an article published in the *Harvard Environmental Law Review* in 2015, writing that such settlement agreements "provide federal agencies with the opportunity to control litigation risk and overcome bureaucratic inertia."[26]

Settlement agreements can require agencies to take a rulemaking action sought by interested parties. Jamie Conrad, a regulatory lawyer, described how this happens in EPA settlements with environmental nongovernmental organizations (ENGOs). In 2015 he wrote in the *Regulatory Review*,

> Obviously, these suits are enforcing congressional deadlines that the EPA has missed. But the EPA has missed a lot of deadlines, and

so the EPA is negotiating much of its workload with ENGOs.... Congress intends the EPA to issue rules when it subjects the EPA to deadlines, but currently, those deadlines end up being recrafted by the EPA, ENGOs, and judges.... Most problematic is the EPA's tendency...to agree in settlements to propose one or more very specific regulatory options in proposed rules.[27]

In essence, agency officials and outside groups sometimes work together to force particular policy outcomes in settling litigation.

Andrew Grossman, a former visiting fellow at the Heritage Foundation, argued that sue-and-settle practices attenuate the influence of elected representatives in policymaking, while empowering outside groups to drive an agency's regulatory action by litigation:

At the most basic level, sue and settle compromises public officials' duty to serve the public interest. Outside groups, rather than officials, are empowered to further their own interests by using litigation to set agency priorities.... At the same time, consent-decree settlements allow political actors to disclaim responsibility for agency actions that are unpopular, thereby evading accountability. Consent decrees also diminish the influence of other executive branch actors, such as the President and the Office of Management and Budget, and of Congress, which may use oversight and the power of the purse to promote its view of the public interest. By entering into consent-decree settlements, an Administration may also bind its successors to its regulatory program far into the future, raising serious policy and constitutional concerns.[28]

The Department of the Interior has a long history of entering into consent decrees and settlement agreements, including some with significant effects on department policy. Between January 1, 2012, and January 19, 2017, under the Obama administration,

Interior entered into over 460 settlement agreements and consent decrees, agreeing to pay upwards of $4.4 billion. In September 2018, I issued an order aiming to mitigate the effects of sue and settle at Interior by increasing public transparency surrounding the department's litigation practices.[29] The order created a publicly accessible web portal for citizens to view information about the department's ongoing litigation, settlement agreements, and consent decrees, while also providing a process for public input before the department approves a settlement with certain long-term policy effects or financial commitments.

The EPA likewise had a long history of sue-and-settle practices. In a 2013 study, the U.S. Chamber of Commerce found that the EPA had entered into agreements in sixty sue-and-settle cases from 2009 to 2012. The updated analysis for 2017 revealed that the agency had entered into another seventy-seven such agreements from January 2013 to January 2017.[30] The settlement agreements between 2009 and 2012 resulted in more than a hundred new regulations, many with more than $100 million in associated compliance costs. The Chamber of Commerce noted in its 2013 study that both advocacy organizations and industry groups had sued the EPA and agreed to settlements with the agency, saying, "Our research found that business groups have also taken advantage of the sue and settle approach to influence the outcome of EPA action. While advocacy groups have used sue and settle much more often in recent years, both interest groups and industry have taken advantage of the tactic."[31]

Sue and settle played a large role in driving the EPA's policy agenda during the Obama administration. The Trump administration then set out to pump the brakes. As the EPA administrator, Scott Pruitt issued a directive in October 2017 to end the practice of sue and settle at the agency. The directive aimed to increase transparency with respect to agency litigation and to stop the practice of regulating through sue-and-settle agreements. "The days of regulation through litigation are over," said Pruitt in a press release. "We will no longer go behind closed doors and use consent decrees and settlement agreements to resolve lawsuits filed against the Agency by special interest groups where doing so would circumvent the regulatory process set forth by Congress."[32] The directive introduced new transparency requirements for agency lawsuits, prohibited consent decrees that exceed judicial authority, and barred attorney's fees and litigation costs from settlements, among other provisions.

The Biden administration, however, has returned agency settlement agreements and consent decrees to the shadows. For example, in September 2022, the administration agreed in court settlements to consider the social cost of carbon emissions in environmental impact reviews for oil and gas leases in Montana and the Dakotas, which is emblematic of using litigation settlements to create new legal obligations for the government that further the administration's policy aims.[33]

The judiciary provides an important check on executive agency power. Judicial deference, however, restrains the judiciary's willingness to determine the law and transfers judicial power to the executive branch. Deference doctrines, which generally direct courts to accept an agency's interpretation of its statutory mandate, serve to limit a significant potential check on their actions.

Congress delegates vast amounts of authority to executive agencies by allowing them to issue legally binding regulations. When legislation is written ambiguously, the agencies that execute the law have considerable leeway to interpret it to their advantage. Within executive agencies, powers of statutory interpretation and regulatory decision making have drifted down to the lowest levels of the civil service, where staff can often put a personal gloss on agency regulations and guidance documents as they apply them. They can take aggressive and arguably tenuous positions against private individuals, with limited review by political appointees. Judges then apply deference doctrines that tilt toward the unreasonable, providing little accountability to the American people.

The Framers divided federal power among three coequal branches of government—executive, legislative, and judicial—to prevent the abuse of power by any single official. Today, legislative and judicial power have shifted into the executive branch, where the three powers intended to be separate are now essentially joined. What can be done about the unchecked exercise of power by administrative agencies? The following chapters propose ways that leadership can better manage the bureaucracy and return policymaking responsibilities to politically accountable leaders.

CHAPTER SIX

THE CHIEF EXECUTIVE

The president, as the nation's chief executive, is tasked with overseeing the implementation and enforcement of all laws. As I experienced during my tenure at the Department of the Interior in two different administrations, presidential approaches to executive branch management can vary widely. Communication with President George W. Bush by a secretary of the interior, for example, required navigating several layers of subordinate White House staff. The experience was often circular and frustrating. President Reagan's first director of the Office of Personnel Management, Don Devine, described his impatience with communicating through White House staff in his chronicle *Political Management of the Bureaucracy*. The "problem with bloated staff," Devine opined, "is not primarily that it costs a lot ... but that staffers get in the way, and do not allow the line operating officers to carry out their missions, at least not effectively."[1] President Clinton's first secretary of labor, Robert Reich, echoed Devine's annoyance in his bestselling memoir, *Locked in the Cabinet*. "Orders from twerps in the White House didn't bother me in the beginning," wrote Reich. "Now I can't stomach snotty children telling me what to do."[2]

In light of the bloated staff of his predecessors, President Trump's approach to the role of chief executive was a breath of fresh air. Gone were the days of twiddling my thumbs as I waited to hear back from White House staff. President Trump himself, at least in my case, relayed his expectations to his cabinet secretaries, who were expected to deliver results. Trump's approach to agency oversight was fundamentally freeing for a cabinet secretary like me who had anticipated having to wait for calls from "twerps in the White House."

Communication with political appointees, whether layered or direct, is just one way that presidents exercise oversight of administrative agencies. The chief executive's toolkit features several instruments of agency oversight that can be used to improve the management of the administrative state. This chapter will examine them in detail, after a brief review of the constitutional basis for presidential authority.

The Foundations of Executive Authority

The president's authority over executive agencies flows from Article II of the U.S. Constitution, which provides that the "executive Power shall be vested in a President of the United States." Thus, it would seem that the "executive Power" of the United States is embodied in the president.

Section 2 of Article II adds some clarification and specifics. For example, it provides that the president is the "Commander in Chief of the Army and Navy of the United States, and of the Militia of the several States." In addition, the president "may require the Opinion, in writing of the principal officer in each of the executive Departments, upon any Subject relating to the Duties of their respective Offices." The president has the power to grant pardons for "Offences against the United States" and, as discussed below, the power to nominate and appoint individuals to federal offices.

Questions of how the chief executive would lead the government predated the ratification of the Constitution itself. *Federalist* no. 70, published on March 15, 1788, is often cited as providing a fuller view of the Framers' thinking when they drafted Article II. In that essay, Alexander Hamilton laid out his vision of a unitary executive:

> Those politicians and statesmen who have been the most celebrated for the soundness of their principles and for the justice of their views, have declared in favor of a single Executive and a numerous legislature. They have with great propriety, considered energy as the most necessary qualification of the former, and have regarded this as most applicable to power in a single hand, while they have, with equal propriety, considered the latter as best adapted to deliberation and wisdom, and best calculated to conciliate the confidence of the people and to secure their privileges and interests.[3]

Hamilton continued by describing the dangers of a multiheaded executive branch. A lack of unity among executive leadership, according to Hamilton, can result in weakened authority and frustrated policymaking:

> Wherever two or more persons are engaged in any common enterprise or pursuit, there is always danger of difference of opinion. If it be a public trust or office, in which they are clothed with equal dignity and authority, there is peculiar danger of personal emulation and even animosity. From either, and especially from all these causes, the most bitter dissensions are apt to spring. Whenever these happen, they lessen the respectability, weaken the authority, and distract the plans and operation of those whom they divide. If they should unfortunately assail the supreme executive magistracy of a country, consisting of a plurality of persons, they might impede or frustrate the most important measures of the

government, in the most critical emergencies of the state. And what is still worse, they might split the community into the most violent and irreconcilable factions, adhering differently to the different individuals who composed the magistracy.[4]

Hamilton's warning of dissension and division within a multi-headed executive branch is all too applicable to the modern administrative state, where far-flung agencies can wield broad powers away from direct presidential oversight and where insulated career staff lack meaningful accountability.

The president has a variety of executive powers to employ in overseeing the executive branch and bringing rogue agencies to heel. These include the president's appointment and removal powers, his authority to issue agency directives, and his oversight of the regulatory review process. Only by harnessing and applying these powers can the president reassert control of administrative agencies in line with the vision of the Framers.

The President's Appointment and Removal Powers

The president's most basic tools for overseeing the executive branch are the powers to appoint and to remove executive branch officers. The appointments clause of the Constitution (Article II, Section 2, clause 2) gives the president the authority to appoint officers of the United States, including cabinet-level department heads and ambassadors. These appointments are subject to confirmation by the United States Senate. Congress can also pass legislation authorizing the president or the heads of departments to appoint inferior officers without Senate confirmation—for example, federal chaplains, federal election supervisors, and certain administrative law judges. Congress cannot waive the Senate's obligation to confirm principal officers.

The Supreme Court clarified the distinction between principal officers and inferior officers in *Edmond v. United States* (1997)[5] and in *United States v. Arthrex* (2021).[6] The court held that only principal officers confirmed by the Senate can issue final decisions that bind the executive branch. Inferior officers must be supervised and directed at some level by a principal officer. A cabinet secretary does not have to review every decision made by an inferior officer but must be able to do so and to overrule decisions. In *Arthrex*, the court held that administrative patent judges (who, despite their name, are members of the executive branch) exercised too much authority to qualify as inferior officers who could be appointed by the agency head without Senate confirmation. The court held that administrative patent judges could be considered inferior officers only if a presidentially appointed, Senate-confirmed official had the authority to review and overturn their decisions. Only the president can appoint agency officials with ultimate decision-making authority.

The appointment power lets the president choose who runs administrative agencies. The president's appointees then set agency agendas, direct policymaking, and limit any agency actions that might run counter to the president's goals. No agencies can take final action without approval from an officer appointed by the president, absent a delegation of the authority to do just that.

The Senate's role in confirming presidential appointees gives lawmakers an avenue to offer feedback on the president's proposed management of the executive branch. This is one of the constitutional checks and balances designed to prevent the concentration of too much power in a single branch of government. While the Senate can check a president's nomination for a political appointment, the president, with a few exceptions, has sole authority to remove his appointees.

The Constitution does not expressly say that the president can remove officers, but the Supreme Court held in the 1926 case *Myers v. United States* that the power to remove presidential appointees generally rests with the president and does not require congressional approval. The court reasoned that the power to remove officials was implicit in the power to appoint them and in the president's duty to faithfully execute the law—a duty that would be undermined if the president had to rely on subordinates in whom he had lost confidence. The court noted James Madison's view on the president's removal power:

> If the President should possess alone the power of removal from office, those who are employed in the execution of the law will be in their proper situation, and the chain of dependence be preserved; the lowest officers, the middle grade, and the highest will depend, as they ought, on the President, and the President on the community.[7]

Notwithstanding the president's general right to remove his appointees, the Supreme Court limited that authority in the 1935 case *Humphrey's Executor v. United States*. William E. Humphrey had challenged his removal from the Federal Trade Commission by President Franklin Roosevelt, citing the provision of the Federal Trade Commission Act that appointees to the commission could be removed only for good cause. The statute specifically defined good cause as "inefficiency, neglect of duty, or malfeasance in office." The court found that Roosevelt's reason for removing Humphrey from his position was political and did not satisfy the good-cause requirement. This ruling set a precedent that allows Congress to give for-cause removal protections to heads of independent multimember federal agencies and prohibits presidents from removing such officers for reasons other than those listed in the controlling statutes.[8]

Since *Humphrey's*, Congress has established a number of independent agencies with principal officers whose for-cause removal protections shield them from direct presidential control. In my view, this framework unconstitutionally insulates independent agencies from oversight by the president and prevents the people's chosen executive from managing agencies' execution of the law. The Supreme Court may also be taking a skeptical stance on the constitutionality of these protections. In *Selia Law v. Consumer Finance Protection Bureau* (2020), the court construed *Humphrey's* to allow removal protections only in agencies that "do not wield substantial executive power." (When the Supreme Court issued its decision in *Humphrey's*, the Federal Trade Commission was seen as acting more in a judicial or legislative role than as an executive agency.)

Consequently, with certain exceptions, when you serve in the executive branch as a political appointee, you almost always serve at the pleasure of the president. You can be asked to leave at any moment, for any reason. That said, political appointees make up a very small fraction of the federal workforce. At the Department of the Interior, we had about 65,000 full-time employees and about ninety political appointees. Across the government, there are about 3,800 political appointees out of 2.2 million civilian federal workers.

Despite the limited number of political appointees available to the president to help guide his policy agenda, there are times when the president's power to appoint or remove officials is called into question. I once found myself in the middle of such a controversy when I was appointed to the International Boundary Commission, U.S. and Canada. This obscure commission was established in 1908 in a treaty between the United States and the United Kingdom on behalf of Canada. Its purpose is to define and precisely mark the boundary between the United States and Canada. It is a very small bipartisan agency that I had not heard of until one evening in the summer of 2007, when I was the solicitor for the Department of the Interior.

I arrived home from work rather late, which was not unusual. As I sat down at the dining table, my cell phone rang. I pulled it out of my pocket and recognized the number of the White House switchboard. Apologizing to my wife, Gena, I stepped into the living room to answer the call.

"Mr. Solicitor," said a man's voice, unfazed by the late hour, "this is the White House Presidential Personnel Office. How are you this evening?"

"I'm well, thank you. How can I help you?"

"We're calling to talk to you about a position as the commissioner of the International Boundary Commission, U.S. and Canada."

"Great," I said, hoping to wrap up the call quickly and have my dinner. "Do you need a reference? You don't even need to tell me about the job. Just tell me who you want to put in the position and I'll tell you what I think of them."

"We aren't calling about a reference, Mr. Solicitor. We're calling about an appointment for you."

I froze. "What do you mean?"

The staffer cleared his throat. "The president intends to appoint you to be the commissioner to the International Boundary Commission, U.S. and Canada."

The silence stretched between us as I racked my brain for a reply. "I'm already the solicitor at the Department of the Interior," I said. "That's a big job."

"Yes, sir. We've talked to the secretary's office and they're very confident that you can do both jobs."

They are? I began to pace the room. "Well, I don't know anything about this job," I said, "and I don't know anything about Canada." My Canadian knowledge at the time began and ended with the fact that my wife was born in Toronto.

"Look," his tone grew frustrated, "the president's going to make this decision tonight."

"What do you mean, tonight?" I stopped short and looked down at my watch. "It's already past eight. The president goes to bed around nine or ten, or so I've heard."

"Yes, and he's making the decision tonight."

I frowned. "Have you talked to the State Department? They might have more qualified people ..."

"We've talked to everybody," he interjected, "and we need to make this decision tonight. We think you're the person we'd like to do it."

What do you say in that situation? You say the only thing you can: "OK."

"Great," he said. "Your commission will be sent over in the morning."

"In the morning? But a commission normally takes weeks to go through."

"In the morning," he repeated. "Thank you."

I hung up the phone and told Gena what had just happened.

She laughed and said, "David, not even this White House will think you should play any role in diplomacy. They will find someone else."

I figured she was right.

To my surprise, when I arrived at my office at Interior the next day, an order from the president was waiting for me on the fax machine. That was not how a normal day in the Office of the Solicitor began.

Then the phone rang. It was the White House Presidential Personnel Office.

"Good morning, Mr. Solicitor. We want to make sure you have received your order to serve as the acting commissioner of the International Boundary Commission, U.S. and Canada. The Department of Justice will call you right away."

"That's great," I said.

When the phone rang again, it was indeed the Department of

Justice. I'd had frequent calls with Justice officials in my role as solicitor and I was used to having an attorney or two on the line. What I wasn't prepared for was an entire team of lawyers. I was puzzled, to say the least.

"Congratulations, Mr. Commissioner," said the assistant attorney general for the Environment and Natural Resources Division of the DOJ. "Would you like our help in seizing your office?"

"Excuse me?"

"Well," he continued, "would you like support to go with you?"

"No," I ventured, wondering what he was talking about. "I think I'll just walk over to the office and go inside. You know, say Hi to the people who work there."

Soon I learned the reason for their concern. It turned out that my predecessor, Dennis Schornack, was not happy about being replaced. Apparently he had gotten sideways with the George W. Bush administration when he told an elderly woman in Blaine, Washington, that she had to tear down a small retaining wall she had built on her property. Shornack believed it encroached into an area known as the vista, a ten-foot-wide zone on either side of the border with Canada. This woman wanted a wall so that her many Pomeranians would not wander onto the street just across the border. She responded to the order by getting a nonprofit law firm, the Pacific Legal Foundation, to seek a declaratory judgment against the International Boundary Commission.

Shornack as commissioner had retained a private counsel to enter an appearance in court on behalf of the commission, and the Department of Justice had not taken kindly to the idea that a private lawyer, rather than the U.S. attorney general, would be litigating for the United States. The dispute between the DOJ and Commissioner Shornack was elevated to the Presidential Personnel Office and ultimately to President Bush, who had Shornack removed from his position. Shornack, however, believed that the president's removal power did not extend to him. The 1908 treaty establishing the commission provided that a vacancy occurred "by reason of the death, resignation, or other disability of a Commissioner." Schornack interpreted this language to be a limitation on the president's ability to remove him from office. The Department of Justice disagreed.

Schornack wasn't there when I showed up at the International Boundary Commission office. I directed that the locks be changed so he couldn't come back, but that didn't stop him from challenging in court the authority of the president to replace him, or from turning up alongside me at official events. For months after his removal, he claimed to be the commissioner of the International Boundary Commission, U.S. and Canada, until litigation finally put the matter to rest in 2010.[9]

Questions still occasionally arise as to the scope and extent of the president's appointment and removal authority, but it remains one of the primary tools that the chief executive can wield to implement his agenda. The selection of active, engaged political appointees is crucial. As Don Devine observed, "political leadership needs to be actively involved in the details of administration or it will lose control of the political agenda for which the election campaign was waged."[10] Presidents should assert their appointment and removal authority to build a team of agency leaders who enthusiastically support the president's vision.

Presidential Directives and Memoranda

In the summer of 2016, a former colleague and friend contacted me to see if I might be interested in serving on the transition team that Chris Christie and his former chief of staff, Richard Bagger, were beginning to pull together for the eventual nomination of Donald Trump. I had previously served as one of the leaders for a similar effort during the 2012 election season, so I agreed to participate.

During my work in this capacity, I began to realize that, should Trump be elected, he would be a consequential president on issues related to the Department of the Interior. As a candidate, he described very specific actions he would take related to conservation steward- ship, energy production, and regulatory change. He emphasized his opposition to the longstanding western Republican orthodoxy of transferring public lands to western states and divesting the federal interest in public lands. He embraced recreational activities on public lands and recognized the conservation achievements led by the hunting and fishing communities. Conservation stewardship and recreation issues were so significant to him and members of his family that the only group I was told to meet with to develop the transition concepts before the election were representatives of American Wildlife Conservation Partners.

Immediately after the election, the transition started in earnest. One of the clear outcomes was the development of various poten- tial presidential memoranda or executive orders. These ideas went through multiple drafting efforts after President Trump was sworn into office. At the beginning of his term, the president issued a series of memoranda and executive orders to lay out an administrative agenda and propel his policy vision. At Interior, we turned these directives into secretarial orders to instruct agency action promptly. These orders expeditiously helped to rectify the heavy-handed regulatory approach toward users of public lands that had plagued the department and had contributed to a workplace culture that no longer served the people.

The prompt issuance of directives, such as executive orders and presidential memoranda, is one of the primary controls a new administration has for steering executive departments in the direc- tion of the president, whose election reflects the will of the people.

Presidents issue directives to the heads of federal agencies to help propel a policy vision through those agencies. Executive orders, though legally binding, are not laws. John F. Kennedy, however, issued an executive order requiring the Department of Justice to review future draft executive orders to ensure that they align with the Constitution and existing statutes.

George Washington issued eight executive orders during his two terms in office, and presidential use of executive actions has increased greatly since then. Franklin Roosevelt issued the most executive orders of any president to date, clocking in at 3,721. While Elena Kagan was a visiting professor at Harvard Law School in 2001, she published a law review article, "Presidential Administration," highlighting a notable shift in the use of presidential directives during Bill Clinton's administration.[11] Kagan noted that President Clinton frequently issued directives to instruct agency heads on a specific course of action, and she observed that directives and memoranda became his primary means of setting and executing his policy agenda. Though previous presidents had also used such directives, Kagan concluded that Clinton's regular and prolific use of these tools represented an innovation in oversight of the executive branch through direct presidential intervention. Subsequent presidents have leaned into that precedent, making the use of directives and memoranda a primary tool in presidential oversight. Political appointees in turn can advance the president's vision by turning executive actions into secretarial orders or similar directives.

For example, President Trump's Executive Order 13771, "Reducing Regulation and Controlling Regulatory Costs,"[12] and Executive Order 13777, "Enforcing the Regulatory Reform Agenda,"[13] directed agencies to reform ineffective, duplicative, and obsolete regulations. Executive Order 13807, "Establishing Discipline and Accountability in the Environmental Review and Permitting Process for Infrastructure Projects," was issued in August 2017. In this order, President Trump established key policy priorities for the federal government, including: (a) safeguard our communities and maintain a healthy environment; (b) ensure that federal authorities make informed decisions concerning the environmental impacts of infrastructure projects; (c) develop infrastructure in an environmentally sensitive manner; (d) provide transparency and accountability to the public regarding environmental review and authorization decisions; (e) be good stewards of public funds, including those used to develop infrastructure projects, and avoid duplicative and wasteful processes; (f) conduct environmental reviews and authorization processes in a coordinated, consistent, predictable, and timely manner in order to give public and private investors the confidence necessary to make funding decisions for new infrastructure projects; (g) speak with a coordinated voice when conducting environmental reviews and making authorization decisions; and (h) make timely decisions with the goal of completing all federal environmental reviews and authorization decisions for major infrastructure projects within two years.[14]

Beyond establishing a policy for the federal government, EO 13807 also contained specific directions for the Department of the Interior. It designated the departments of the Interior and Agriculture as the lead agencies for facilitating the identification and designation of energy right-of-way corridors on federal lands for government-wide expedited environmental review for the development of energy infrastructure projects. It required that Interior provide the Office of Management and Budget with a "strategy and recommendations for a multi-agency reorganization effort."[15] And it directed that "federal agencies should follow transparent and coordinated processes for conducting environmental reviews and making authorization decisions."[16]

Perhaps most noteworthy, it established that "the time for the Federal Government's processing of environmental reviews and authorization decisions for new major infrastructure projects should be reduced to not more than an average of approximately 2 years, measured from the date of the publication of a notice of intent to prepare an environmental impact statement or other benchmark deemed appropriate by the Director of OMB."[17] Previously, an environmental impact statement under the National Environmental Policy Act (NEPA) could take as long as twenty or more years to develop and could run to thousands of pages that no one could honestly read.

In response to EO 13807, as deputy secretary, I promptly issued Secretarial Order (SO) 3355 to implement a streamlined process for infrastructure and energy projects in accordance with the president's directives and to initiate an assessment of additional improvements that could be made to further facilitate the president's objectives.[18] This order recognized that the purpose of NEPA's requirements was not the generation of paperwork but the adoption of sound decisions based on an informed understanding of environmental consequences. I emphasized that the regulations encouraged agencies, among other measures, to: 1) focus on issues that truly matter rather than amassing unnecessary detail; 2) reduce paperwork, in part by setting appropriate page limits; 3) discuss briefly issues that are not significant; and 4) prepare analytic (rather than encyclopedic) documents. I then directed the agencies to strive to meet certain page and timing goals to further the policy the president had adopted. In short, President Trump laid out his policy vision and the leadership of Interior took action to implement his vision.

President Joe Biden later adopted this bullish approach to presidential management to set his policy agenda. Within his first month in office, he issued more than thirty executive orders instructing agency action. Many of these actions repealed policies issued under the Trump administration and directed administrative agencies to act on a new set of policy priorities. One area of particular focus was departing from the Trump energy policy. Among other things,

President Biden directed a pause on oil and gas leases on federal lands and on the outer continental shelf. Within six months, a federal court issued a preliminary injunction on actions taken by the secretary of the interior to carry out this order. The United States District Court for the Western District of Louisiana found that the State of Louisiana and other states were likely to prevail in their claims that only Congress, not the executive branch, had the authority to pause oil and gas leases.[19] In August 2022, the district court issued a permanent injunction on the Biden administration's pause of oil and gas leasing. Among other things, the court found that the Department of the Interior had failed to comply with the Administrative Procedures Act in attempting to carry out the president's order.[20]

The president does not actually have to sign an executive order or a presidential memorandum to tell his appointees to do something. He could just pick up the phone and convey his views to them. And President Trump often did that. But executive orders and memoranda have an additional benefit beyond demonstrating presidential action: they tell political appointees and career staff—up and down the bureaucracy—exactly what the president wants to be done. This direction lightens the burden on agency political appointees by spelling out the president's clear intent. An executive order ends the internal executive branch debate about how and whether to make a policy change.

The effective use of executive actions can aid a president in propelling his agenda through the agencies of the executive branch. Political appointees can follow up with secretarial directives that implement the president's policies at the agency level. But they need to be careful to dot their "i"s and cross their "t"s so they don't cause embarrassment for the president, as occurred with some of the early actions that the Biden administration took relating to energy policy at the Department of the Interior that were rejected by federal courts.

The President's Regulatory Review Authority

A very fortunate day in my tenure as deputy secretary of the Department of the Interior was over a month before I would be sworn into office. June 29, 2017, was the day that Neomi Rao was confirmed by the Senate to serve as the administrator of the White House Office of Information and Regulatory Affairs (OIRA) in the Office of Management and Budget (OMB). Why did this matter to me? Because the major duties of any deputy secretary include working with various OMB offices to resolve issues identified in the interagency regulatory review process (where multiple agencies comment to OIRA on other agencies' proposed regulations), develop the president's annual budget submission, and prepare congressional testimony and reports. Ineffective political leadership of OIRA, and of the OMB at large, can turn these processes into a nightmare, while good leadership greatly helps deputy secretaries and other political appointees implement the president's policies.

Regulatory review, in the context of the chief executive, refers to the president's authority to oversee the regulatory actions issued by administrative agencies in line with the president's agenda. It may involve an examination of the content or implications of a rule, its estimated costs and benefits, or adherence to procedural requirements. Through retrospective regulatory review, presidents can determine if existing regulations should be retained, changed, or rescinded. The Office of Information and Regulatory Affairs is tasked with managing the president's regulatory review process. Theoretically, if OIRA finds that a rule departs from the president's priorities, the office can instruct agency staff to make changes. Agencies, in turn, occasionally withdraw rules from the rulemaking process when faced with White House opposition. Regulatory review allows a president to keep a close eye on agency rulemaking and instruct agencies to change course when appropriate.

President Jimmy Carter and President Ronald Reagan both issued executive orders to implement their vision of the regulatory review process, but President Bill Clinton's Executive Order 12866, "Regulatory Planning and Review," is now the guiding standard for regulatory review practices.[21] Issued in 1993 and designed to guide presidential oversight of regulatory and administrative policy, EO 12866 governs federal agency rulemaking, regulatory planning, and regulatory review. Most notably, it governs how agencies conduct cost-benefit analysis in the rulemaking process and heightens transparency through the public release of documents related to the regulatory review process. The order also authorizes OIRA to review all regulatory actions, whether new or preexisting, that are deemed "significant," having an economic impact of $100 million or more.

Elena Kagan observed in "Presidential Administration" that President Clinton's approach to regulatory review was more aggressive than that of his predecessors. EO 12866 put forth a model of presidential oversight of the administrative state that tightened the president's authority over the discretionary power of his political appointees. "[T]he fairly clear premise of the order," wrote Kagan, "was that the simple delegation of rulemaking authority to a specified agency head (the kind of delegation which underlies almost all regulations) would not prevent the President from making a final decision." Whereas President Reagan and his predecessors had not asserted any direct power to overrule the decisions of agency officials, Clinton did so. According to Kagan, such authority reduced the need for the president to exercise the removal power. "Under this view," she observed, "the President would not need to resort to his power of removal over executive branch heads to ensure a certain rulemaking result: that result would—or at least should—follow by virtue of a presidential (displacing a secretarial) order."

Subsequent presidents have generally followed in Bill Clinton's footsteps on regulatory review. George W. Bush issued executive orders making adjustments to the EO 12866 framework, but left the Clinton model largely intact. Barack Obama later revoked Bush's orders and reaffirmed the Clinton approach to regulatory review. Thus, EO 12866 endures as the overarching framework for presidential oversight of the regulatory process. Through robust regulatory review practices, a president can gain a firm grasp of agency activity and exert his authority over the discretionary powers of agency heads.

My view of the application of the president's authority over the regulatory review process differs slightly from Kagan's. While she suggests that presidents exert control over regulatory review mainly through directives to the heads of rulemaking agencies, I believe that the president theoretically has a lot of authority over the regulatory review process through his political appointees at the OMB—if he chooses to use it. Unfortunately, the OMB career bureaucracy has often captured the process, especially on the programmatic analyst side. Instead of furthering the president's policies, the program specialists drive their own agenda. To overcome such personal agendas requires the executive agency to have its own political appointees engage with those at the OMB, which can be hit or miss. If that initial engagement doesn't work, the executive agency either gives up or continues to raise the issue to higher political levels until it is resolved, possibly by the president. This effort wastes a great deal of administration leaders' time and energy.

During my tenure in the Bush administration, I saw major regulatory priorities of the secretary of the interior completely torpedoed in OIRA's review process even after it was made clear that they were presidential priorities. This experience made me uneasy about implementing President Trump's regulatory agenda when I was back at the Department of the Interior again. I was acutely aware that the president had communicated a vision of empowering the private sector as well as state and local governments by reducing unnecessary and burdensome regulations, to unleash American ingenuity and economic growth.

Luckily, progress in reducing regulatory burdens at Interior had already been made through our collaboration with Congress to enact legislation under the Congressional Review Act (CRA) early in 2017. The CRA enables Congress to pass a joint resolution of disapproval to overturn a new federal agency rule and block the issuing agency from creating a similar rule in the future. By this means, Congress had disapproved burdensome rules that were perceived to be regulatory overreach by the Obama administration. Congress's use of the CRA avoided imposing needless regulatory burdens on the American public and freed up the administration's time to address other areas of focus. Going forward, we targeted the following regulatory and deregulatory priorities:

- Promoting American energy development and energy independence.
- Increasing outdoor recreational opportunities for all Americans.
- Enhancing conservation stewardship in ways that strengthen the economy or minimize burdens on it.
- Improving management of species and their habitats.
- Upholding trust responsibilities to the federally recognized tribes and Alaska natives by addressing their economic development challenges.

Given the expectation to move with dispatch on the regulatory front, I viewed Neomi Rao's confirmation to lead the OMB's Office of Information and Regulatory Affairs as highly fortuitous. I had previously worked with her when she served in the White House Counsel's office during the George W. Bush administration. The Department of the Interior was part of her agency portfolio then, so she would understand the department's issues. I knew that she would be fair to everyone in the process of reconciling the varied comments she would receive from other departments on Interior's regulatory proposals. She would also recognize how important timely action was to achieve the president's policy outcomes. Most importantly, I believed that she would be able to ensure that her staff in OIRA's Natural Resource and Environment Branch were kept on task. My expectations were borne out.

In the first two years of the Trump administration, Interior was able to confer with Rao, agree upon priorities and schedules, and move forward at an expeditious pace. Interior has a small regulatory footprint by comparison with that of agencies such as the Department of Labor or the Department of Health and Human Services, but it was a leading executive branch agency for regulatory reform during the Trump administration. Much of our success was the result of Rao's efficient and accessible leadership at OIRA, which facilitated the regulatory review process.

The Office of Management and Budget is effective only when its political leadership holds the staff accountable, to ensure that policy reflects the president's view. For the president's part, the tool of regulatory review is only as effective as the president and his political appointees make it.

White House Czars

When things go wrong in government, people usually demand that a single person be put in charge. That's why presidents often assign an informal advisor to manage major challenges or initiatives. Such an advisor or task force leader is sometimes referred to as a "czar," a word that derives from the Russian pronunciation of Caesar and was made famous under the doomed Romanov dynasty. After President Woodrow Wilson appointed Bernard Baruch as head of the War

Industries Board, the American press dubbed him the first industry czar. The term stuck, and so did the practice. Presidents have used czars and other such informal advisors regularly since World War II.

President Trump used this approach in appointing Vice President Mike Pence to lead the White House Coronavirus Task Force, and President Biden did likewise in appointing Vice President Kamala Harris to manage the challenges associated with immigration. Czar-led task forces have typically met with mixed success, but the intent is to achieve better coordination and drive outcomes more quickly than cabinet agencies might do.

President Biden has also brought former cabinet secretaries and subcabinet leaders into the White House to manage key initiatives and coordinate policy actions. For example, Gina McCarthy, former EPA administrator, was made the national climate advisor and led the National Climate Task Force. John Kerry, former secretary of state, serves as the special presidential envoy for climate. This method places the equivalent of principal officers who are essentially attempting to direct agency operations within the confines of the White House, without imposing on them the burden of Senate confirmation. It sets up an administrative structure that functions outside the normal agency review process. By focusing operations in the White House, it may also circumvent applications of the Freedom of Information Act and the Inspector General Act, thereby avoiding processes that have become increasingly weaponized to interfere with executive decision making. Biden's approach is a vigorous effort to coordinate and manage the cabinet agencies and drive their progress with a multitude of czars.

———————

Most modern presidents have tried to exert more control over administrative agencies, with varying degrees of success. Naturally they want to use the tools in their toolbox to achieve the goals they laid out to the American people. From my perspective, President Trump's open communication with members of his cabinet marked an effective shift in the management of the executive branch. The president's use of the available tools can help move his agenda forward in the face of an entrenched and intransigent bureaucracy.

CHAPTER SEVEN

DRAINING THE SWAMP

It's early afternoon on a beautiful day in June 2020 and I'm at a beach on the Gulf Coast of Florida. The sun reflects brilliantly against the deep water, but I'm not focused on the scenery as I return to my government vehicle. Instead of listening to the sound of the waves tumbling along the shoreline, I've got two sentences (or one sentence, with emphasis) running on repeat in my head. I just asked an endangered species expert at the Fish and Wildlife Service what her job was, and she earnestly replied, "I speak for the mice! I speak for the mice!"

That declaration was cemented in my brain for the rest of my tenure as secretary of the interior. It encapsulated my greatest concern regarding our nation's government: well-meaning employees who advocate for their own pet cause rather than serving as neutral, technically competent administrators. This employee was passionate about her job and excited about her work, but her passion was not tethered to the law underlying her job. Instead of approaching her work with the neutral administrative competence at the heart of the merit based civil service, she appeared to be a zealot for protecting mice. In her view, the law tasked her with "speaking for the mice" as their advocate. But that was not actually her job. Her job was far more nuanced: faithfully executing the authority that Congress, through the Endangered Species Act, had granted to the secretary of the interior. Hearing her answer, I was skeptical that she had ever read the law she was tasked with administering.

The ESA granted specific authority to the secretary of the interior for the purpose of safeguarding endangered species, such as ensuring that they are not illegally taken, preventing federal agencies from acting in ways likely to jeopardize their continued existence, and protecting their habitat. The law doesn't have a provision that says "serve as a relentless advocate." This employee either did not understand the balances and limitations written into the text of the ESA, or chose to ignore them. For me, her statement represented the fruit of the longstanding failure of political leaders of both parties to guide agency decision making in accordance with the law and to hold civil service members accountable for their job performance.

When political leadership is unwilling to hold career staff accountable, functionaries who are neither elected nor appointed can wield power in a thick swamp of regulatory and enforcement actions. These individuals often feel free to follow their own tune, doing what they personally think is right instead of adhering to the words of the law or the policy direction of agency political leaders. In this chapter, we look at some possible ways that agency leadership and Congress can drain the bureaucratic swamp of entrenched freelancers and restore accountability to the executive branch.

An Unmoored Office in the Executive Office of the President

During my time at Interior, one of the worst and most recurrent examples of bureaucratic freelancing I encountered was from career staff at the Office of Management and Budget. The agency's Natural

Resource Programs office (particularly the employees at the Interior Branch and the Water and Power Branch) frequently appeared to be working at cross-purposes with the president's policy direction. Simply put, the OMB's longstanding career budget examiners often seemed to have decided that *they* set policy, rather than the secretary, agency officials, or the president. Their freelancing was often purported to be done in keeping with the intent of the president— someone that many of them had never spoken with—while they resisted any proposal that was not in accordance with their own personal views. Because of their intransigence, issues often needed to be raised directly to OMB political appointees. In some instances, political appointees were willing to work to resolve issues once they were convinced of the need to align with the president's vision. But in many cases, the political appointees were not interested in making tough decisions or leading their own subordinates.

It turned out that I was not alone in my frustration with OMB staff. I was aboard Marine One in 2019 right after President Trump had taken much criticism about the budget proposal he had sent to Congress that recommended cutting the federal government's approximately $18 million in funding for the Special Olympics. As the president boarded the helicopter, he was a bit hot. He said that he had called the secretary of education, who had explained that the OMB—not the Department of Education—had recommended the funding elimination. When he asked the head of OMB the reason for this decision, the answer was basically that it was part of a scoring scheme and that Congress would just put the money back in. The president then essentially told the head of the OMB that his name was on the budget and that doing stupid things to play stupid budget games did not make sense. As the president vented his frustration, I thought of how much that message would hearten every cabinet secretary who had received biting criticism from Congress for a stupid budget submission made by an OMB employee.

The president has a tremendous opportunity to drive his agenda through the OMB, but the opportunity is often squandered as soon as the president's political appointees start to turn the details over to entrenched career staff in the Executive Office of the President. That being said, President Trump's appointees at the OMB, as well as the Office of Personnel Management, recognized the problem of career staff embedding their own policy goals into federal decisions, and they made an effort to address some systemic issues in the civil service. These efforts might have led to a more accountable bureaucracy if President Trump had served a second four-year term.

Rein in Union Abuses and Hold Poor-Performing Employees Accountable

Few things are more important to securing representative government than making improvements to our civil service system. Since my public service ended, I have served as the chair of the Center for Freedom at the America First Policy Institute, where along with James Sherk, the center's director, I have focused on holding the bureaucracy accountable. It is critical to our nation that policymakers build upon the work that President Trump initiated in 2018 when he issued Executive Orders 13836, 13837, and 13839 for the purpose of creating a more efficient and accountable civil service. EO 13839 aimed to streamline the processes for disciplining and dismissing poor performers. In theory, federal merit system principles require agencies to dismiss underperforming employees who cannot or will not improve.[1] In practice, that rarely happens. One major reason is that it takes agencies a lot of time and effort to dismiss a poor performer, and the employee has a decent chance of getting reinstated on appeal. Agencies therefore try to remove only the worst of the worst, usually letting mere underperformers slide.

Federal law mandates some of the procedures that make removals difficult. Others were created by regulation, administrative case law, collective bargaining agreements, or internal agency practices. EO 13839 was designed to remove the added obstacles to dismissing poor-performing employees and enable agencies to do what Congress expressly instructed them to do.[2]

For example, the Civil Service Reform Act (CSRA), passed in 1978, established a new process to make it easier for agencies to remove poor performers from the job, codified in Chapter 43 of the United States Code.[3] But agencies almost never used it, dismissing only a couple of hundred employees or so through the Chapter 43 process each year.[4] Instead, they mostly used the pre-CSRA firing process set out in Chapter 75.[5] The main reason appears to be that individual agencies had added their own policies and procedures onto the Chapter 43 removal process, imposing more burdens than the law mandated.

Chapter 43 requires agencies to give poor performers "an opportunity to demonstrate acceptable performance," better known as a Performance Improvement Period (PIP).[6] These PIPs typically last two to four months.[7] Many agency union contracts also require a Performance Assistance Period (PAP) before a PIP begins. PAPs typically last one to three months. Supervisors must work extensively with the poor performers during PAPs and PIPs. But the CSRA said nothing about how long PIPs last and nothing at all about PAPs. Executive Order 13839 directed agencies to lift these extralegal impediments to removing poor performers, limiting most PIPs to thirty days and eliminating PAPs altogether. The result was to make the Chapter 43 process easier to use, as Congress intended.

EO 13839 also addressed some Merit Systems Protection Board (MSPB) decisions that made it very difficult to remove employees for misconduct. The MSPB generally requires supervisors to administer discipline consistently: if a supervisor lets most employees go with a reprimand for a particular infraction, the supervisor as a rule cannot fire another employee for the same offense. Historically, the MSPB would look to employees with the same supervisor doing similar work as "comparator" employees when evaluating discipline. Under the Obama administration, the MSPB decided that it would consider any employee in the same agency to be a comparator.[8] This forced agencies to apply consistent discipline across the agency, which could range from a few thousand employees to well over a hundred thousand. If a supervisor anywhere in the agency gave an employee a reprimand or suspension for a particular offense (say, bringing drugs into the workplace), then the MSPB wouldn't let anyone in the agency fire another employee for the same offense.

This made it very difficult for agencies to fire anyone for misconduct, since employees could often find someone, somewhere in the agency who had done something similar and not been fired. In one case, the Transportation Security Administration (TSA) tried to fire an air marshal who was arrested for soliciting a prostitute in Hawaii. His arrest caused him to miss the flight he was assigned to cover the next day. The MSPB decided that the TSA could not fire him because it had not dismissed another employee involved in an altercation at a brothel in Germany (where prostitution is legal).[9]

In another case, the MSPB ruled that the U.S. Postal Service could not fire an employee who brought cocaine onto agency property, was arrested for doing drugs in an alley next to her facility during a lunch break, and was subsequently convicted. The MSPB held that the Postal Service could not fire this employee because it had not fired another employee for drug-related offenses.[10] The Obama-era MSPB used any previous leniency for similar conduct anywhere in an agency as grounds to overturn removals.

Nothing in the CSRA required this standard, and it was counterproductive. EO 13839 directed the Office of Personnel Management to clarify by regulation that the Obama-era MSPB got it wrong. It specified that only employees doing similar work in the same work unit—not across the whole agency—were appropriate comparators in dealing with a particular kind of misbehavior.

In addition, EO 13839 ended what is often known in the federal government as the "dance of the lemons." When an agency is removing an employee for poor performance or misconduct, the employee not infrequently agrees to resign instead of getting fired. But there is a catch: in exchange for the employee semivoluntarily leaving and forgoing the (extensive) rights of appeal, the agency agrees to wipe the employee's disciplinary record clean. The dismissal is entered on that person's official employment record as a voluntary departure, not a termination.

In isolation, these "clean record settlements" make sense for individual agencies, allowing them to get rid of a particularly bad apple without expensive litigation. But they have terrible effects government-wide. The not-technically-fired employees often simply jump to other agencies. The new agency has no idea that the employee in question was a lemon. It doesn't show up anywhere in the employee's wiped-clean personnel file. The previous agency has committed not to share that information during reference checks. For the new agency, it is much easier to hire someone who has already served in the federal government than someone from outside.[11] Bad employees therefore often circulate between agencies rather than leave the government entirely.

EO 13839 put an end to this destructive "lemon dance." It prohibited agencies from wiping employees' disciplinary records clean. If an employee was being fired for poor performance or misconduct but resigned before the termination took effect, the agency would be required to share that information with other federal agencies.[12] This way, the agencies would know if they were hiring a lemon.

Executive Order 13836 targeted collective bargaining activities.[13] Federal law requires agencies to pay the salaries of both their own negotiators *and* the union's bargaining team.[14] Agency union contracts also usually require paying for union travel expenses. These subsidies give unions every incentive to take their time, and federal union contract negotiations typically drag on for years. The Department of Veterans Affairs (VA), for example, began negotiating its primary union contract in 2003 and didn't complete negotiations until 2011. The Office of Personnel Management reported that federal agencies spent roughly $16 million on salaries for union negotiators in 2016.[15]

EO 13836 aimed to streamline this lengthy and often wasteful collective bargaining process so that negotiations could be completed in less than a year. It required agencies to make union contracts publicly available online. The order also created an interagency Labor Relations Working Group to facilitate communication among agencies engaged in collective bargaining. If one agency found a particular union contract provision to be onerous or unworkable, it could share that information across the government through the working group. Other agencies would then know not to make the mistake of agreeing to similar language. Incredibly, agencies did not do this before President Trump!

Executive Order 13837 sought to curb abuses of taxpayer-funded union time—an arrangement that allows federal employees to work for a federal union while on the clock at an agency. Many federal employees don't do any agency business; they spend all their working hours doing union business. For example, prior to EO 13837, almost five hundred VA employees worked entirely for a union and did no patient care.[16] At the same time, there were long waiting lists for care at many VA facilities. Federal agencies spent $177 million in taxpayer funds on union time in 2016.[17] Federal law requires agencies to give unions some taxpayer-funded union time, but EO 13837 limited employees to spending no more than a quarter of their duty time doing union business. It forbid agency employees from lobbying on taxpayer-funded union time. Previously, agencies effectively paid unions to lobby Congress—often lobbying against the administration's policy priorities! EO 13837 prevented agencies from granting union time to pursue grievances; the federal government would stop paying unions to contest employee dismissals.

The order also required agencies to stop being wasteful with taxpayer-funded union time. Some agencies granted enormous amounts of union time, while others ran a tighter ship. EO 13837 directed agencies to aim for government best practices: no more than one hour of taxpayer-funded union time per fiscal year for each employee the union represented. At Interior, we were already below this level, so the order did not affect our operations greatly.[18] But many other agencies were much more profligate and had to rein in their spending on union time. Government-wide, this directive would reduce union time use by about two-thirds.

Federal unions reacted to Executive Orders 13836, 13837, and 13839 as if the sky were falling. The National Treasury Employees Union (NTEU) called them "a threat to federal employees."[19] The head of the American Federation of Government Employees (AFGE), J. David Cox, attacked the orders as "a direct assault on the legal rights and protections that Congress has specifically guaranteed."[20] (Cox later resigned from AFGE amid charges of corruption and sexual harassment.)[21] In fairness to the unions, the executive orders did undercut their bottom line. Taxpayers had been giving federal unions hundreds of millions of dollars in union time and other subsidies. The orders meant that unions would have to cover those costs themselves, leaving them with a lot less money to spend on politics and lobbying—or, for J. David Cox, to spend (allegedly) on unnecessary limousine services.[22]

Of course, saying "Trump is driving a hard bargain and getting taxpayers a better deal than Obama did" is not a particularly compelling criticism. Instead, unions attacked the orders with over-the-top histrionics. Yet the federal employees they claimed to speak for appeared to like these orders. Shortly after they were issued, the Government Business Council conducted a poll asking federal employees if they supported or opposed the "administration's efforts to make it easier to fire poorly-performing employees." Respondents said they supported these efforts by a 2-to-1 margin.[23] The federal government's longstanding failure to address the problem of under-performers was actually frustrating to other federal employees. The Federal Employee Viewpoint Survey showed that federal employee job satisfaction rose after President Trump signed the orders, hitting a record high in 2020.[24] Moreover, the proportion of federal employees believing that their agency effectively deals with poor performers rose from 29 percent in 2016 to an all-time high of 42 percent in 2020.[25]

Unsurprisingly, both Republican and Democratic members of Congress pushed back against the changes. A group of twenty-one Republican members of the House of Representatives sent a letter to Trump requesting that he rescind the executive orders.[26] A group of twenty-three Democratic House members sent the president a similar letter. The status quo of the swamp has defenders in both parties.[27]

The swamp also struck back: AFGE, NTEU, and several smaller federal unions filed lawsuits against the orders, claiming they violated the Civil Service Reform Act. Their claims were largely unpersuasive. On the merits, the CSRA protected the president's authority over the executive branch and gave him broad discretion to act. Procedurally, the Supreme Court has held that parties generally need to challenge agency decisions through administrative channels before going to federal court.[28] This meant that the unions were first supposed to challenge the implementation of the executive order with the Federal Labor Relations Authority (FLRA).

The unions' case was assigned to Judge Ketanji Brown Jackson at the district court for the District of Columbia. In August 2018, Judge Jackson issued an injunction preventing the Trump administration from implementing the orders. She determined that the president didn't have the authority to issue them and that the unions didn't have to go through administrative channels first.[29] Her ruling temporarily prevented the administration from implementing key parts of the orders.

The administration promptly appealed. A year later, a panel of the United States Court of Appeals for the D.C. Circuit (including judges appointed by presidents of both parties) unanimously lifted Judge Jackson's injunction. The appeals judges ruled that Jackson was wrong to allow the unions to go directly to federal court, holding that they had to go first to the FLRA.[30] The unions asked the full D.C. Circuit Court to reconsider the panel's decision. Not a single one of those appeals judges thought Jackson had ruled correctly.[31]

The unions tried bringing suits in other courts, too. The Service Employees International Union (SEIU) filed suit before an Obama-appointed district court judge in New York. She ruled against the unions on the same grounds as the D.C. Circuit.[32] SEIU appealed to the United States Court of Appeals for the Second Circuit. A panel with judges nominated by presidents of both parties rejected their arguments.[33] The National Association of Agriculture Employees (NAAE) sued against the orders in Maryland. Another Obama-appointed district court judge ruled against them.[34] Finally the issue came before the FLRA, which held that the president had the authority to issue the orders.[35] In total, seventeen federal judges heard union challenges to the executive orders—eleven appointed by Democratic presidents and six appointed by Republicans. Ketanji Brown Jackson was the only one of those judges to rule against the orders, but her injunction prevented the Trump administration from implementing them for over a year.[36]

Improve Accountability of Agency Policymakers

Facilitating the removal of poor-performing career agency employees and drawing a hard line against collective bargaining abuses weren't President Trump's only efforts at revitalizing the civil service. He also aimed to restore the accountability of career agency staff who serve in policy-influencing roles. Trump explained that he considered poor performance by employees in policy-influencing positions to be especially problematic; it can impair agency effectiveness and sabotage key policy initiatives.[37] He issued a new directive intended to strike a balance between holding career agency staff in policy-influencing roles more accountable and maintaining their distinction from political appointees.

In October 2020, President Trump issued Executive Order 13957, which directed federal agencies and the Office of Personnel Management to reclassify federal civil service employees who serve in policy-related roles, such as regulation writers and policy planning staff, as members of a newly created Schedule F in the excepted service. Employees in Schedule F would have the same removal appeal rights as political appointees, which is to say they would not have any.[38] However, the order required agencies to implement internal procedures to ensure that Schedule F employees were not hired or fired based on their politics. The order kept these policy-influencing career positions nonpolitical while letting agencies quickly fire employees who filled them. The order applied to career employees in "confidential, policy-determining, policy-making, or policy-advocating positions."

Federal unions reacted as expected. AFGE called it "the most profound undermining of the civil service in our lifetimes.... President Trump has declared war on the professional civil service."[39] Opponents argued that the order would politicize a large portion of the civil service. According to AFGE's new national president,

Everett Kelley, "This executive order strips due process rights and protections from perhaps hundreds of thousands of federal employees and will enable political appointees and other officials to hire and fire these workers at will."[40]

In reality, the Schedule F executive order represented an effort to return to the foundations of the civil service. The Pendleton Civil Service Reform Act of 1883 prohibited agencies from hiring or firing career employees based on their political views, but agencies enforced those requirements internally. Employees did not have a right to the lengthy external appeals that made termination difficult. As we saw earlier, the civil service reformers intentionally left federal employees at-will. They wanted to put an end to the patronage-based spoils system, but they never intended to insulate policy-influencing employees from accountability.[41] EO 13957 gave agencies the ability to remove poor-performing or unmanageable employees from policy-influencing positions while protecting them from adverse personnel decisions based on their personal political affiliation.

Democratic lawmakers and unions nonetheless pushed back. Shortly after taking office, President Biden rescinded EO 13957 as well as EO 13836, EO 13837, and EO 13839, arguing that the orders undermined the merit system protections of the civil service and impeded collective bargaining. According to Biden, the creation of Schedule F in particular "not only was unnecessary to the conditions of good administration but also undermined the foundations of the civil service and its merit system principles, which were essential to the Pendleton Civil Service Reform Act of 1883's repudiation of the spoils system."[42] President Biden directed OPM to reverse its regulations aimed at streamlining the dismissal process for poor-performing employees and required agencies to renegotiate their union contracts to reinstate provisions that make it harder to fire federal employees.[43] He rolled back the Trump administration efforts to bring efficiency and accountability to the civil service.

Federal employees do not seem happier having returned to the status quo. The Federal Employee Viewpoint Survey, which reached an all-time high in 2020, registered a five-point drop in job satisfaction scores in 2021—the largest one-year drop on record, and lower than at any point under the Trump administration.[44] Despite this backward momentum, President Trump's civil service executive orders provide a template for reconstructing and reenergizing the civil service to make it efficient and responsive to the expressed preferences of the American people.

Besides the civil service changes put forth by Trump through executive action, I think there would be merit in considering the benefits and challenges of moving to at-will employment for all federal employees. Far too many in the civil service—like Dr. Deborah Birx—have abandoned the role of neutral, nonpartisan, professional and effective administrators, instead promoting policies of their own choosing, as long as they aren't caught. At-will employment could help return accountability to a system that assumes the civil servant is a neutral professional administrator who will take policy direction and proceed forward. Making federal employment statutorily at-will would restore the original vision for the merit service. As the Civil Service Commission explained in 1913, the policies underlying the Pendleton Act and the Lloyd–La Follette Act "at all times left the power of removal as free as possible, providing restraints only to ensure its proper exercise." At-will employment, moreover, can function in tandem with prohibitions against firing based on political affiliation or preferences. Under this framework, agencies could terminate employees for any reason except those prohibited by law, such as racial discrimination, just as private businesses do in removing poor-performing employees.[45]

Put the Government Closer to the People It Serves

The sagebrush ecosystem extends across eleven western states and two Canadian provinces. Over 60 percent of the ecosystem is on public lands, half of which are managed by agencies within the Department of the Interior, primarily the Bureau of Land Management (BLM).

A high-level political appointee once told me the story of a senior career BLM official based in Washington, D.C. The career official had just explained to the political appointee how excited he was to travel out west and have a chance to see sagebrush.

"Sage grouse?" I asked, thinking the political appointee had meant to refer to the large bird native to the sagebrush ecosystem. "That's great."

"No," he said, "I actually mean he was excited to see sage*brush*!"

I was stunned. The BLM manages 245 million acres and much of that area constitutes a sagebrush ecosystem. The fact that the senior career official had never seen the dominant ecosystem he was tasked with administering struck me as a notable illustration of how disconnected the agency decision makers were from the effects of their decisions on the ground. Another example of that disconnect occurred when a D.C.-based team of career staff took the lead in an effort to rewrite grazing regulations. BLM officials in the field reviewed the draft and reported back to the main office that the regulations made no sense. The agency's D.C. staff were far removed from the experience of agents in the field. These incidents and many others like them convinced me that our nation's government experts should work much closer to the people they serve, in locations where they can better understand the activities and issues connected with their responsibilities.

In my view, the growth of the federal government has resulted in a senior career federal workforce that is increasingly distanced from its mission of serving the American people. Much like ivory-tower academics, senior career executives and policymakers entrenched in the D.C. bubble often fail to comprehend the real effects of their policies at the grassroots level. Relocating government actors outside the Beltway—closer to the problems they address and the people they serve—is one solution we implemented at Interior to remedy this disconnect. But it was not embraced by all of the senior career leaders who enjoyed the trappings of important positions in the nation's capital, nor by some of their predecessors who had gone on to serve as consultants to the entities they formerly regulated.

Even before he was confirmed to serve as secretary of the interior, Ryan Zinke was determined to improve the department's organization and possibly move the headquarters of various subagencies out of Washington, D.C. President Trump subsequently issued Executive Order 13781, which required the director of the OMB to propose a plan to reorganize government functions and programs. Relocating agencies outside the capital made sense as a fiscal matter, since it would reduce costs to the taxpayers as well as living expenses for federal employees. For example, when I eventually moved the BLM headquarters to Grand Junction, Colorado, the difference in cost of living meant that a federal employee's locality pay was 13 percent higher in D.C. than in Grand Junction. Besides lowering costs, relocating to Colorado would bring the people in the headquarters closer to the issues faced by the people in the field offices.

The assistant secretary tasked with leading Interior's reorganization did a phenomenal job, but some agency staff kept their heads down, hoping that the reorganization effort would stall and fade away. From my perspective, the senior career staff of the BLM did virtually nothing to act on Zinke's vision for two years. When I took the helm of Interior in 2019, I asked BLM staff for their plan to relocate the headquarters and was told that none existed, even though the lease on their current office space had an end date that was rapidly approaching.

It was disappointing to see that the BLM had invested so little thought in the secretary's priority, yet the lack of planning actually gave me the opportunity to reevaluate the whole project. I saw little reason for many of the positions then in D.C. to be located there. For example, the leadership of the Wild Horse and Burro Program sat in Washington, but there are no wild horses or burros running around the capital city. The leaders of the BLM's training programs had their offices in D.C., even though the agency's National Training Center was in Phoenix. I also didn't foresee much benefit from simply plucking the Wild Horse and Burro staff from D.C. and putting them in another places that wasn't anywhere near those animals. I wondered if the potential relocation was an opportunity to locate these "experts" closer to the various resources they were responsible for managing.

I came to see that a major benefit of relocating the headquarters would be the opportunity to develop centers of excellence for various functions that the bureau carried out in key states. BLM mining expertise, for example, could be located in a state that had substantial mining activity. Then the "experts" could actually drive from their office to a mine site. This would also minimize the disconnect between employees at headquarters and those in the field. To me, the relocation was not only about where functions are performed, but about how agency staff can better respond to the needs of their colleagues and of the people they serve.

The relocation would also allow for placing employees where they could better support the functions of the state offices in western regions, which bore the largest burden of work within the bureau. The top-heavy structure of the D.C. headquarters was depriving these offices of human resources they needed to function effectively. Shifting critical leadership positions and supporting staff to western states—where the great bulk of federal lands are located and where the majority of leadership actually wanted to be—would result in a better management system, to the benefit of the people in western communities.

I gave the BLM senior career staff a timeframe to determine the optimal location for each headquarters staffer, and informed them that if they didn't bring me a workable plan within that time, I would make those decisions myself. It took an ultimatum for them to recognize that change was inevitable. I thought these career executives had let their staff down by choosing not to initiate a serious administration priority, which meant they had to develop and implement a plan in a far shorter timeframe than they had originally been given.

The bureau analyzed each position currently devoted to headquarters-specific functions both in Washington, D.C. and in the field. Under the plan implemented, about sixty of these positions would continue to be based in Washington, where their functions were logically located. They included a majority of the staff whose duties were tied to budgetary matters, as well as most of those working in the Legislative Affairs, Regulatory Affairs, Public Affairs, and Freedom of Information Act divisions. Approximately 222 positions currently serving headquarters functions in Washington would perform the same duties in locations throughout the western regions, to optimize the bureau's presence where the needs were greatest. Given the need for more technical experience in the field, 74 headquarters positions, some of which had been vacant for several years, were reallocated to work closer to state offices and their duties would be realigned to meet immediate priorities. For example, analysts who had worked on preparing environmental reviews under the National Environmental Policy Act at the D.C. headquarters would be placed in state offices to help their environmental documentation and planning. Finally, the BLM director, deputy director of operations, assistant directors, and a few members of their staff would be relocated to Grand Junction, Colorado, as part of the initiative to establish a western headquarters. When the relocation was accomplished, the new headquarters brought the agency's expertise closer to its employees in the western states.

In September 2021, my successor as secretary of the interior, Deb Haaland, announced her intention to return the national BLM headquarters to Washington. In September 2022, Tracy Stone-Manning, the bureau's director for the Biden administration, explained that the agency was "moving critical positions back to Washington, DC, and anchoring a headquarters presence in Grand Junction, Colorado," with specifics on the staffing to be developed later.[46] The next day, a newly organized chapter of the National Treasury Employees Union formally notified the bureau that "federal labor statutes require the agency to negotiate with the union over the terms and conditions" of the announced relocation plan.[47] Apparently, at least some of the employees then located in the West found it preferable to the D.C. swamp.

Many federal agencies have a similar structure, with a D.C. headquarters, regional or state offices, and local offices. Given the benefits of the BLM relocation, agency leaders now or in the future might study this example and consider how a realignment could better serve the public. The widespread use of teleworking during the coronavirus pandemic demonstrated that federal employees do not all need to be physically located in the nation's capital for agencies to function effectively. Nearly half of federal employees teleworked every day while Covid-19 was raging.[48]

Bringing the government closer to the people doesn't only mean physical proximity, however. Government agencies can take advantage of technology to empower citizens to engage with them more easily and meaningfully. President Biden issued an executive order along these lines shortly after he assumed office, directing specific agencies to improve their customer experience and encouraging agencies to better coordinate services.[49] This is a step in the right direction to help the federal government serve the public more effectively. There are additional ways to think about improving efficiency of service: How might an agency be differently aligned to better serve the American people? Do we even need all the functions that the federal government fills today? These are questions that each agency's political leadership and Congress should be asking.

Place Accountability for Agency Decisions Squarely on the Shoulders of Political Appointees

Far too often, agency decisions are made by career staff, and then political appointees wash their hands of responsibility. Even conscientious political appointees may be hesitant to overrule decisions made by career staff, fearing charges of improper political interference. To foster greater accountability, decisions of significant magnitude should be made by presidentially appointed, Senate-confirmed officials (PAS). Enforcement actions and fines above a certain threshold, for example, should always have to be issued by a PAS within the agency. Likewise, agency expenditures and grants above a certain amount should be made only by senior political appointees. Under such a standard, the decision maker is accountable to the American people through the president.

Agencies can also be made more responsive to the American people by means of an office specifically established to receive and address complaints by members of the public regarding abuses of the regulatory enforcement and adjudication processes. Such complaints could be limited to procedural violations, such as violations of the implementing regulations and policies of President Trump's Regulatory Bill of Rights. Agency heads should task the offices with assessing whether a violation occurred, preparing a plan for remediation where such a violation occurred, and reporting assessments of alleged violations to the agency head. Currently, Americans facing out-of-control administrative agencies have little recourse unless they can afford to take the agency to court—a very expensive proposition.

Each Cabinet Department Should Issue
Its Own "Rule on Rules"

A large portion of my tenure at Interior was focused on driving toward a more balanced regulatory paradigm in response to President Trump's issuance of Executive Order 13771, "Reducing Regulation and Controlling Regulatory Costs," and Executive Order 13777, "Enforcing the Regulatory Reform Agenda." We developed and issued regulations intended to foster responsible onshore and offshore energy development, prioritize worker safety, expand outdoor recreation and conservation, strengthen cultural resource protections, and support tribal economic development. We engaged in dozens of deregulatory actions estimated to bring more than $5 billion in savings to taxpayers.[50] One goal I was unable to fulfill was adopting a regulation similar to the so-called "rule on rules" implemented by the Department of Transportation (DOT).

Under Secretary Elaine Chao's leadership, the DOT assertively responded to the president's executive orders. One action that Secretary Chao took was to codify regulations for the department's rulemaking, guidance, and enforcement actions, partly in response to a petition from the New Civil Liberties Alliance seeking the promulgation of "regulations prohibiting departmental components from issuing, relying on, or defending improper agency guidance."[51] This is what became known informally as the "rule on rules."

The rule on rules enhanced transparency in how the DOT issued rules and guidance documents, and it strengthened due process in enforcement actions. The rule codified the Trump administration's "2-for-1" regulatory budgeting reform. It established policies to ensure that any regulations imposing burdens were narrowly tailored to address statutory mandates or identified market failures, and that they specified performance objectives when appropriate. The rule prescribed the procedures that the department had to follow for all stages of the rulemaking process, including the initiation of new rulemakings, the development of economic analyses, the contents of rulemaking documents, their review and clearance, and the opportunity for fair and sufficient public participation.

Importantly, the rule on rules codified the DOT's procedures for the review and clearance of guidance documents. Before they could be issued, these documents had to be reviewed to ensure that they did not impose any substantive legal requirements beyond those in statute or regulation. If a guidance document purported to describe, approve, or recommend specific conduct beyond what existing law required, the guidance must include a statement explaining that it did not have the force and effect of law and was not meant to bind the public in any way. The rule recognized that guidance documents, though not legally binding, can nonetheless have a substantial economic impact on regulated entities or cause them to alter their conduct, and therefore it mandated a good-faith cost assessment of the consequences of the guidance.

The rule on rules clarified the department's procedural requirements governing enforcement actions to ensure that they satisfied principles of due process and remained lawful and reasonable. In particular, "due process" for any party that is subject to an agency enforcement action includes "adequate notice of the proposed agency enforcement action and a meaningful opportunity to be heard by the agency decision maker."[52] The rule established a policy that the conduct of agency employees "must be fair and free of bias and should conclude with a well-documented decision as to violations alleged and any violations found to have been committed."[53] Beyond setting a clear enforcement policy, the rule mandated that all enforcement actions must have a clear legal foundation, where the authority to prosecute an asserted violation or the authority to impose monetary penalties "must be clear in the text of the statute." Absent a specific regulation or statute to the contrary, "the proper forum for the enforcement action is Federal court, and the enforcement action must be initiated in court by attorneys of the Department of Justice acting in coordination with DOT counsel."[54]

The rule on rules addressed longstanding concerns about the lack of notice provided to the public in advance of enforcement actions, and required that "all documents initiating an enforcement action shall ensure notice reasonably calculated to inform the regulated party of the nature and basis for the action being taken to allow an opportunity to challenge the action and to avoid unfair surprise."[55]

Finally, the rule on rules required the approval of counsel for any proposed settlement agreement, consent order, or consent decree that would "impose behavioral commitments or obligations on a regulated entity that go beyond the requirements of relevant statutes and regulations, including the appointment of an independent monitor or the imposition of novel, unprecedented, or extraordinary obligations...."[56]

The DOT's rule on rules should serve as a model for other cabinet agencies in a future administration to follow. Likewise, Congress should consider using it as a starting point for codifying a rule to provide the public with important protections from the actions of any executive branch agency. Its broad adoption could go a long way toward draining the worst parts of the swamp.

Develop General Permits
for Most Regulated Activities

A great deal of the power of federal employees flows from their ability to refrain from acting unless or until they choose to. One example is delaying or withholding permits for citizens to do things that require discretionary approval. Permission by federal regulators is needed under countless laws and regulations for a wide range of activities, including alterations to one's own property. Congress has woven a complex tapestry of statutes with differing procedural requirements that federal agency employees must comply with before a permit may be granted, and has given scant attention to improving those procedures. Federal agencies have developed permit programs with little thought to whether they are efficient in meeting the needs of the public. Having spent decades working with federal agencies, I can assure you that they are not. As the scope of federal permitting has expanded, the permitting processes have become lengthier and less predictable.

Our nation's federal agencies are failing to grant timely approval or disapproval to permit applications for infrastructure projects—for example, in transportation, electricity distribution or transmission, renewable energy development, mining, fossil fuels production or refining, and natural gas or oil pipeline transmission. The uncertainty of infrastructure permitting drives investment away from these projects. In addition, there is considerable uncertainty that a federal permit will survive judicial review after it is granted. Legal uncertainties and resulting delays impair the nation's ability to respond to challenges associated with drought, wildfire, and the protection of precarious species.

The permit review process is formally initiated when a federal agency receives an application for a permit to authorize a specific activity. (Completing the application is itself a process that can take years and countless informal meetings with the agency.) Once a completed application is received, the agency begins its required procedural processes, which often include compliance efforts under a variety of laws such as the National Environmental Policy Act, the Endangered Species Act, and the Historic Preservation Act, among others. To comply with each statute, the agencies navigate a different set of procedures that may involve diverse federal agencies and bureaucrats. These processes too can take years. The White House Council on Environmental Quality (CEQ) recently reviewed the length of time it takes federal agencies to prepare an environmental impact statement (EIS) under the National Environmental Policy Act. This review found that the process was taking much longer than the CEQ had anticipated in 1981, when it estimated that completing an EIS under its regulations, even for a complex project, should take no longer than a year. But in 2019, the CEQ found that, across the federal government, "the average time for completion of an EIS and issuance of a ROD [record of decision] was 4.5 years and the median was 3.5 years."[57] Over one quarter of the EISs took more than six years to complete.

The length of time the agency review process can take and the unreasonable requirements that agency staff may attempt to impose for getting a permit can cause great frustration for applicants. I once explained to an agency staffer that a proposed permit condition was illegal, and her response was that my client needed a permit and would not be getting one without the condition she required, legal or not.

One possible way to improve the permitting structure is for agency administrators or Congress to establish a standard or prerequisite that any potential applicant for a given type of activity can just comply with rather than go through the lengthy and uncertain process of applying and waiting for discretionary action by an agency official. To do this, either Congress or agency administrators would develop "general permits" or "permits by rule" for particular categories of action.

Congress has provided authority for a federal agency to issue general permits on a national, regional, or state basis in limited circumstances, such as under the Clean Water Act. To date, general permits have been restricted to relatively low-impact activities in certain areas that result in minimal adverse effects, such as the development of boat ramps, access roads, or culverts. As long as an entity's activities stay within the general permit criteria, its actions are compliant. In other situations, Congress has authorized the use of "permits by rule," which apply to similar activities within a designated category. As part of its efforts to regulate air quality, for example, the Environmental Protection Agency issues permits by rule for comparable emissions units or sources in specific areas, such as auto body repair shops or dry cleaning services.

While the specific control mechanisms and requirements differ for general permits and permits by rule, the goal is the same: to reduce unneeded burdens on both the regulatory agency and the applicant, while maintaining consistent health, safety, or environmental standards. General permits and permits by rule minimize the ability of freelancing agency employees to add arbitrary, burdensome, and sometimes unlawful requirements to permit terms and conditions. They eliminate opportunities for agency officials to prevent an action by not granting a permit. Congress and agencies could greatly improve the regulatory process by further promoting the development of general permits or permits by rule.

Congress or a thoughtful agency administrator should require agencies to develop public requirements for conditions that must be met if certain activities can proceed. The permittee can go forward upon committing to meet those conditions, and would be held accountable for acting in violation of the requirements. A prospective permittee who wishes to deviate from a generalized process could file a specific permit request and be subject to the bureaucracy's whims.

Congress Should Evaluate Whether the Programs They Created Are Achieving the Intended Results

Federal agencies are capable of managing the level of accountability demanded by the political leadership or by Congress. Regrettably, little accountability is actually demanded by either. Few political appointees enter office with much understanding of the substantive law, procedures, or internal authorities for agency decision making. Few in Congress are committed to evaluating whether the programs they have authorized and funded are delivering the outcomes they were designed to achieve. Every government program has a constituency that supports it, and those constituencies come out of the woodwork the minute it looks like a change in the program will be proposed. They are typically focused on obtaining money for their projects, not shuttering projects. As a result, few in Congress seriously examine the operations and outcomes of programs they are funding.

The congressional authorizing committees that establish programs usually have little to say about a program's success or failure once it is enacted—absent a media scandal, a Government Accountability Office report, an inspector general's report, or a budget submission that reduces funding. The relevant appropriations committees are often focused on funding their own pet programs through marginal increases in existing programs or the development of "pilot" programs. The congressional appropriations committees are often not aligned with the authorizing committees. Consequently, when the statutory authorization for a program has expired and the program is no longer authorized in law, the appropriators keep funding the expired program anyway. When this is done, the appropriation itself is viewed as a congressional authorization under the law, so the program simply continues.

For decades, various legislators and members of think tanks have called for sunset provisions to force Congress to revisit federal laws or regulations, but such legislation has not become law. One action a new majority in Congress could take to begin to tackle the massive backlog in expired programs is to deem any proposed appropriation for a program that is not currently authorized in law to be subject to a point of order in the House of Representatives, which would allow a single member to stand up and strike the program. A more modest approach would tailor such a rule change to apply the point of order only at the request of the chair of the authorizing committee. Many expired programs are popular, just not so popular that anyone wants to make the effort to reauthorize them. The efficacy of this approach would therefore come down to political will in Congress—which is precisely why the status quo persists.

Congress Could Change How the Executive Branch Regulates

The Congressional Review Act (CRA) of 1996 set up a mechanism that allows Congress and the president to check federal agency rulemaking by passing a resolution of disapproval to overturn certain agency rules and prevent the issuing agency from putting a similar rule in place in the future. Since the enactment of the CRA, many legislative proposals for modifying regulatory activity in the executive branch have been put forward by members of Congress from both parties. None have been enacted, though many have real merit. The proposals range in focus and scope, but each provides an opportunity for Congress to change how the executive branch operates:

- Senator James Lankford (R-OK) and Senator Kyrsten Sinema (D-AZ) have promoted two bipartisan proposals for regulatory improvement. The first of these is the Early Participation in Regulations Act, which would direct agencies to issue advance notice of rules costing more than $100 million annually.[58] The second is the Setting Manageable Analysis Requirements in Text (SMART) Act, which would require agencies to set metrics for how a rule will be measured for success in the future and use those metrics to review the rule within ten years.[59]

- The Regulations from the Executive in Need of Scrutiny (REINS) Act would require major rules to be approved by Congress before they could take effect.[60]
- The Regulatory Accountability Act (RAA) would revise the definition of a major rule and create a new tier of regulations known as high-impact rules.[61] It would define major rules primarily as those with an annual economic impact of at least $100 million and high-impact rules as those with an annual economic impact exceeding $500 million (with those thresholds updated for inflation every five years). Both types of rules would receive additional scrutiny prior to promulgation, including increased standards for the assessment of costs and benefits and a requirement for the consideration of viable alternatives made available for public comment. In addition, an agency would be required to adopt the regulatory alternative that maximizes net benefits, unless the administrator of the Office of Information and Regulatory Affairs approves another alternative. High-impact rules would be subject to an extra layer of scrutiny. Once such a rule is proposed, anyone would be able to petition the agency to hold a public hearing to hash out factual disputes over the agency's justification for the rule. The hearing would include testimony and cross-examination, resulting in an official decision either upholding the agency's original factual basis for the rule or requiring modification. Other major provisions of the RAA include allowing new administrations to recall midnight rules (those issued in the last 60 days of an outgoing administration) submitted to the Federal Register but not yet published; requiring that interim final rules be finalized, modified, or rescinded within 180 days; and extending cost-benefit analysis to

guidance with an economic impact of $100 million or more annually.

- The Small Business Regulatory Flexibility Improvements Act (SBRFIA) would expand the Small Business Advocacy Review (SBAR) panel process to other agencies.[62] The SBAR panel process allows small businesses and organizations an opportunity to offer their perspective on certain proposed rules. The legislation would empower the chief counsel of the Small Business Administration's Office of Advocacy to write regulations on federal agency compliance with the Regulatory Flexibility Act (1980). SBRFIA would also require agencies to consider both direct and indirect costs and benefits to small businesses.
- The Searching for and Cutting Regulations that are Unnecessarily Burdensome (SCRUB) Act would establish a Retrospective Regulatory Review Commission made up of outside experts who would develop a list of regulations to repeal. That list would then be sent to Congress for an up-or-down vote.[63]
- Congress could place a limit on the net cost of a federal agency's regulatory space by setting a specific cap on the economic cost of an agency's regulations. This is commonly referred to as setting a regulatory budget.

Each of these legislative proposals would bring more accountability back into our system of government. Members of Congress should seriously examine their merits.

Congress Could Minimize
Third-Party FOIA and IG Abuses

Minimizing the weaponization of the Freedom of Information Act (FOIA) and inspectors general would help steer the government toward a path of strengthened political accountability. Both Republican- and Democrat-aligned groups use FOIA nonstop to pummel political appointees in the executive branch. They file a massive number of FOIA requests aimed at forcing agency leaders to spend valuable time on document searches. More importantly, such requests are designed to find a nugget of information to target political opponents in a press release. FOIA is a valuable tool for government transparency when used appropriately, but I believe it is frequently abused as a means to slow down policymaking and distract political appointees from their policy agenda. Given modern electronic storage systems, if Congress wants true transparency, perhaps Congress should require that the administrative record for all federal decisions be placed on the web after a decision is made.

FOIA application is limited to the executive branch; it's not a burden that either Congress or the courts have to contend with. You can't FOIA a member of Congress and see what he's thinking about an issue (though if you could, it might be enlightening), nor can you FOIA judges. In a nutshell, the executive branch is subject to a weapon that doesn't touch the other arms of the government. The abuse of serial FOIA requests has a chilling effect on agency communications, since staff become reluctant to use email. The goal of transparency is laudable if it serves a public purpose, but that purpose would be equally well served if the law were applied to the communications of Congress and the courts too.

The same premise applies to inspectors general (IGs). Interest groups and politicians have weaponized the filing of complaints with IGs as a routine part of their media strategy. Once a complaint is filed, it often sets off a cascade of effects from a communications perspective. The department's chief of staff gets involved, senior staff look at the factual scenario, and other senior staff talk to the ethics or legal experts to examine the conduct of the employee, which takes a great deal of time and attention. All of these effects occur independently of the actual IG investigation, which can take months or even years to wind through the system. During that time, the people who filed the complaint are pummeling the accused individual in public by saying the person is under a cloud of suspicion—which may never be lifted. The IG investigation may be resolved without a report, or it may not be resolved until long after the individual has left office.

The lack of neutrality among investigators in the IG's office can also be jaw-dropping. While I was the solicitor at Interior during the Bush administration, Secretary Kempthorne often tasked me with resolving issues with Interior's inspector general, Earl DeVaney. During the eight years of the Bush administration, Earl carried out numerous high-profile investigations that caught the attention of the media and Congress. He had a captivating personal story and a larger-than-life persona. As a result, he was highly regarded within the IG community. During Kempthorne's tenure, Earl and I worked closely together to such an extent that we kept in touch after I left Interior and he retired. In fact, he was one of the few people I called to ask for advice before I decided to submit my name for consideration to serve as deputy secretary in the Trump administration. His guidance served me well through my entire tenure as deputy secretary and secretary.

In the early spring of 2006, I was given a draft report from the Office of the Inspector General that evaluated whether the subject of the investigation had violated government gift rules. After I reviewed the report, I was provided with information that appeared to demonstrate that one of the investigators had posted substantial material hostile to George W. Bush on his website. I subsequently met with Earl and his team and explained that his investigator's public criticism of the Bush administration created an appearance of bias. Earl acknowledged the problem, but told me he had known the investigator's father from his service in another agency, and essentially said "the kid's an idiot and his father was a friend of mine." The investigator appeared to modify his website soon afterward, yet

I had to wonder if he could be fair and neutral in any investigation that was initiated by partisan complaints from Congress. When I returned to the Department of the Interior a decade later, Earl had retired and "the kid" was still there, handling a myriad of new duties in high-profile investigations. Every time I became aware that he was involved in an investigation related to allegations about a political appointee, I wondered whether someone I viewed to have once been a partisan advocate would be an impartial investigator.

An appearance of bias becomes especially concerning when you realize that a report from the inspector general will be taken as gospel by the media and often by many in Congress, even though the person who is the subject of the investigation has no opportunity to correct the record before the report is issued. Once a report is published, whether it is factually correct or not is largely irrelevant in the court of public opinion.

In brief, these are some strategies for draining the swamp: Agency officials should read the actual law they have been tasked with administering and focus the agency's efforts on implementing the law to a T. Congress should take action on complex policy decisions, monitor congressionally created programs more effectively, and enact legislation to improve the regulatory process. These suggestions, together with political appointees who are willing to lead, can help restore accountability to executive branch agencies.

CHAPTER EIGHT

DRIVING CHANGE AS A POLITICAL APPOINTEE

I was smiling when I exited my government-issued Suburban driven by a dedicated security detail, strode to the White House entrance, and headed upstairs to the West Wing. I had an idea that could help both the White House and the Department of Defense meet one of the president's goals related to the construction of the border wall.

I took my seat at a conference table in a room filled with a cast of characters from various offices of the White House, the Department of Defense (DOD), the Department of Homeland Security (DHS), and the Border Patrol. Mick Mulvaney, the White House chief of staff, led the discussion about the anticipated progress and potential delays in the border wall construction.

In February 2019, President Trump declared a national emergency regarding border security and the humanitarian crisis along our southern border. Later in the year, DOD announced a decision to defer $3.6 billion to fund eleven barrier projects at the border. As part of that effort, DOD was considering applying for an emergency transfer of administrative jurisdiction of approximately six hundred acres of federal land from the Department of the Interior to the Department of the Army to build roughly seventy miles of border barriers. Both DOD and DHS were concerned that Interior's processes would interfere with their mission and timetable.

It was my understanding, going into the meeting, that someone at Army had convinced superiors that it would take a year to complete the process of transferring administrative jurisdiction. The attorneys in the Office of the Solicitor at Interior had assured the Army, the DOD, and the DHS (among other agencies) that it would not require a year, but these agencies decided to elevate the issue and complain that the effort was going to take longer than the White House anticipated. The three agencies apparently indicated to the White House that Interior's process made their job impossible. I had reviewed the law on transfer of jurisdiction, examined the Bureau of Land Management's implementing regulations, and conferred with Interior's lawyers. There was no real problem that would need a year to resolve, but I thought we could accelerate the timeline with a bit of help from the DOD. First I would need to get a ride in a Blackhawk helicopter.

I suggested that if the Army submitted emergency applications, I would personally conduct a site inspection, reviewing the situation at each requested site along the southern border. This kind of review would normally have been handled by BLM field offices, but in this case I proposed doing it myself. I would be able to evaluate the situation on the ground directly, and I could then generate the documentation rendering a decision. This would be much more expeditious than moving the process through the bureaucracy at the usual glacial pace. To complete the review of any applications promptly, I asked the military to provide me with access to a helicopter.

The Department of the Army submitted its emergency applications and gave me a ride in a Blackhawk. Soon I was visiting the sites over which the Army requested administrative jurisdiction. I observed the challenges facing our dedicated staff along the border concerning immigration control, drug enforcement, and natural resource values, and saw the risks posed to national security if the military did not move forward with the construction of the wall.

If you are a political appointee carrying out your oath of office, you need to be always striving to propel the president's agenda, after taking care to understand your legal authority. It is important to understand how to leverage your authority to meet the president's goals lawfully. At times this requires a bit of creativity, but it is incumbent upon agency leaders to bring solutions to the White House, not problems. At the end of the day, an agency leader's approach to unexpected challenges is the real test of success or failure. This chapter records some of the biggest takeaways from my experience as a political appointee and suggests a path for reinstating effective political leadership in the bureaucracy.

The Role of a Political Appointee in a Federal Agency

Under the law, political appointees are the supervisors of the executive branch. For example, Congress charged the secretary of the interior with "the supervision of public business" relating to the department's subagencies (the National Park Service, the Bureau of Land Management, the Fish and Wildlife Service, the United States Geological Service, and the Bureau of Indian Affairs, to name a few), the U.S. Territories, petroleum conservation, public lands, and a host of other items.

Political appointees fall into two categories: principal officers and inferior officers. The Constitution's appointments clause governs the method of appointment for both types of officers. The Supreme Court case *Morrison v. Olson* (1988) clarified that cabinet-level department heads, ambassadors, and federal judges qualify as principal officers who are constitutionally required to be appointed by the president and confirmed by the U.S. Senate. Other officers, known as inferior officers, do not require Senate confirmation and can also be appointed by agency heads or the federal courts.[1] These officers include multiple levels of political appointees in agencies that Congress created, such as deputy secretaries, assistant secretaries, undersecretaries, and bureau directors. Federal employees, unlike political appointees, are not required to be appointed according to the appointments clause, and they exercise less authority under the law.

Each new law passed by Congress tasks a political appointee, often a cabinet officer, with carrying out the various responsibilities contained in the law. Given the volume of work that Congress has tasked to political appointees, agency heads delegate authority to inferior officers and to agency employees. A few officials at Interior, such as the deputy secretary and the solicitor, have broad general delegations. For example, the solicitor was delegated the authority to exercise all of the secretary's legal powers within the department, among other specific delegations. Some officials have narrower delegations. Each agency official in turn may subdelegate authority to other officials in the organization.

In *Buckley v. Valeo* (1976), the Supreme Court specified that an officer, unlike an employee, "exercises significant authority pursuant to the laws of the United States." This means that political appointees, not agency employees, have the ultimate say on substantive policy decisions.[2] A lower-level employee in an agency is therefore exercising some authority that has flowed down from an agency head or other high-ranking official, but has no authority otherwise. It is the responsibility of political appointees to supervise all subordinate staff in the exercise of their delegated authority, not just defer to an employee's view.

As the federal government has grown over time, the number of career agency employees and contractors has exploded. The vast majority of tasks undertaken by administrative agencies today are carried out by career staff. Legally, those staff are exercising authority delegated to them by a political appointee, who always retains the option of carrying out the task personally. One example is when I inspected federal lands near the border wall construction myself.

Just as career employees often don't grasp the limits of their authority, political appointees don't always appreciate the magnitude of their own responsibilities. Some arrive at the agency believing that their role is simply to pass whatever is prepared by the career staff on to the next step in the decision process. They view themselves as figureheads riding on a ship that will move forward even if they don't put much of their shoulder into the wheel. In reality, each appointee has signed up to discharge their duties "well and faithfully" and to be an agent of change on behalf of the president. That takes a great deal of effort.

Successfully driving change in the executive branch requires a lot of learning and engagement on the part of political appointees. At times, appointees fail to realize that they have been charged with the obligation to oversee a multitude of different subject areas. They also fail to recognize that they must personally review and understand their legal authority. They should not trust anyone else to explain their authority to them until they have read the relevant statute, regulation, or manual themselves. One of the most embarrassing moments I ever witnessed in a professional setting was when a political appointee came into a meeting with Gale Norton, then secretary of the interior, and proceeded to explain why she could not take a certain action based on the National Park Service Organic Act, only to have Secretary Norton—who had previously served at Interior as the associate solicitor for parks and wildlife, the top lawyer for the National Park Service—explain that the Organic Act did not actually say what the appointee had asserted. The political appointee had accepted without question what her subordinates told her, and it was flat-out wrong.

There are essentially three types of political appointees in the federal government: those hired into Schedule C positions, those hired as noncareer Senior Executive Service (SES) members, and presidentially appointed, Senate-confirmed (PAS) employees. The Senate confirmation process can be arduous for anyone. Even before that point, a host of issues can slow or stall an individual's nomination. In the Trump administration, for instance, the Federal Bureau of Investigation seemed to be stymieing the background review process. Once a person was nominated at the assistant secretary level or below, it could be a drawn-out personal nightmare. One of our nominees at Interior was reported unanimously out of committee in the Senate, only to be held up by the Democrats from floor consideration for over two years.

PAS employees (and some non-PAS employees) generally have line authority, which is drawn from specific delegations by the department secretary or through the law itself. Authority in an agency flows through general and specific delegations from the cabinet officer down. However, the vast numbers of Schedule C and noncareer SES political positions are devoted to serving as advisors to PAS appointees and do not actually have the legal authority to direct an agency employee to take a particular action. It is important that both the political appointee who serves as an advisor and the appointee's supervisor with line authority understand this in dealing with the agency career staff.

Transitioning a Campaign to a New Administration

In the early days of the Trump administration, I thought the president's team did a great job of quickly taking on some high-profile campaign commitments. By issuing executive orders and memoranda shortly after taking office, President Trump helped to ensure that the various departments would quickly act on his priorities. This strategy was developed during the transition and implemented in the early days of the administration. For example, members of Interior's transition team facilitated the department's prompt response to these orders and memoranda by developing a plan to draft secretarial orders to set the president's directives in motion, and by working closely with the broader transition policy team to ensure consistency with the president-elect's vision. In the end, the Interior team submitted a nearly sixty-page plan to the president's transition leadership, providing a framework for first-term priorities based primarily on commitments the president had made on the campaign trail. Following the transition, the team of political appointees who entered executive agencies (commonly referred to as "beachhead teams") took varied approaches to advancing the president's agenda. At Interior, the beachhead team developed secretarial orders that awaited Secretary Zinke's confirmation. After he was sworn in, he promptly issued the orders.

My experience in the Bush administration had been very different. From my perspective as a junior staffer, it did not appear that there was a meaningful plan of priorities until the summer of the first year of President Bush's term. At Interior, the administration waited many months for the political appointees to be assembled before taking on a host of policy issues. Unfortunately, when the machinery of a federal agency is put on pause, it takes a great deal of effort to put it back into gear. Equally unfortunate, the Bush administration officials were thrown off their agenda by the terrible events of September 11, 2001. At Interior, moreover, a bitter lawsuit related to the management of individual Indian account funds dominated leaders' attention over all other policy issues. Key takeaways from my experience in the early days of the Bush administration were the importance of having clear policy goals on day one and the need to begin driving change as soon as possible.

While still a nominee for secretary of the interior during the transition to the Trump administration, Ryan Zinke generally embraced the conceptual agency action plan developed by the transition and expanded it to include his vision for a major departmental reorganization. When he arrived in office in March 2017, Zinke's actions largely encompassed the priorities of the agency action plan. For example, he began his first day in office by issuing secretarial orders to tee off the president's directive and address conservation stewardship issues. His willingness to greenlight much of what the transition team had developed, coupled with the fact that many of the team members eventually served at Interior, meant that the department's appointees were basically on the same policy page and were able to implement change faster than many of their predecessors. That said, the Interior appointees during the Trump administration waited for Zinke's confirmation before issuing substantial policy actions. The Biden administration's Interior Department initiated some major policy directives even before Deb Haaland was confirmed as secretary, which added time back to the administration's term.

Having clear direction and policy consistency in the early days of the Trump administration was tremendously beneficial. To this end, the composition of the beachhead team mattered greatly at an agency like Interior, where only about 0.001 percent of the employees are political appointees. In setting up Interior's beachhead team, the goal was having roughly equal parts campaign staff, individuals recommended by the nominee for secretary, and people who had previously served in the department. I felt strongly that representation from people who knew the department's processes and many of the career personnel they would be dealing with was critical to giving the administration a chance to be successful early on. Drawing upon experienced individuals sends a clear message of competence to the career ranks. It can also avert a lot of testing by career staff who may be opposed to the policy view of the incoming administration. Several members of Interior's transition team subsequently entered the department through the confirmation process, which helped ensure policy consistency and further supported the president's ability to drive change.

The portion of the beachhead team made up of experienced agency staff must possess the skills most needed by the secretary in the early days of an administration. There is always interest in whom the secretary will pick to work in the crucial roles of his immediate office, but it is the experienced staff who can expeditiously make the wheels of government turn. For a policymaker to have a significant influence on, for example, a revised budget for the next fiscal year, that person must have staff capable of quickly identifying problems and making use of existing processes to implement change effectively.

At Interior, the beachhead team designated an outstanding member of the political staff—known in many of the department's bureaus as an extraordinarily competent administrator—to exercise the authority of the deputy secretary through a secretarial order on day one. This action signaled to the entire agency that we were serious about moving forward promptly. That individual passed away in 2021, and his funeral service was filled with former political appointees (from the Reagan, George H. W. Bush, George W. Bush, and Trump administrations) as well as many career staff, including the security guard for the department's parking garage. That is the type of person you want in a position to assist a newly minted secretary at the start.

Since the massive agencies of the federal government largely run on autopilot unless active leaders take charge, the leadership of the transition and beachhead teams must be sure that political appointees have clear direction not only on how to staff offices but also on which offices to staff in order to achieve control of key agency functions. Political appointees must gain an understanding of the flow of agency processes to ensure that the views of the current administration are reflected in everything the agency generates from the first day until the last.

Once the beachhead teams have landed in their respective federal agencies—shortly after noon on Inauguration Day—they will likely be expected to move with great dispatch on a number of fronts. Often the White House chief of staff or the acting director of the Office of Management and Budget will promptly distribute guidance for first-day activities, such as extending the effective dates of not-yet-effective regulations and halting the publication of materials in the Federal Register pending review. The directions may sometimes be hit-or-miss, so the beachhead team might feel like it's in a holding action. In any case, each beachhead team should quickly secure control of the agency's Executive Resources Board, which is responsible for the management of Senior Executive Service members, and begin a thoughtful consideration of how to adjust the staffing of the department's top management to reflect the priorities of the new administration.

The Biden administration moved rapidly on its policy initiatives starting on the first day. For example, on January 20, 2021, the career official exercising the authority of the secretary at Interior suspended the delegation of authority for a wide variety of activities, such as: (a) the publication of items in the Federal Register, including actions related to the National Environmental Policy Act; (b) the issuance, revision, or amendment of resource management plans; (c) the granting of rights-of-way, easements, or any conveyance of property, as well as any notices to proceed under previous surface-use authorizations of ground-disturbance activities; (d) the approval or amendment of plans of operation; (e) the issuance of any decision with regard to certain rights-of-way or disclaimer of interest; and (f) the appointment, hiring, promotion, or approval of the appointment of anyone to a position above the level of a GS-13.[3] Given this assertive precedent, I think it reasonable to expect that the next incoming administration will want to replicate the Biden administration's urgency.

In addition to moving fast on its policy initiatives, the Biden administration was hostile to the continuation of Trump appointees on various advisory boards. Such appointments are generally for set terms. During the two administrations I served in, the policy was to let the term expire and then allow the president or secretary to fill the position, rather than asking people to resign before their term was completed. That comity changed with the Biden administration, which aggressively removed term appointees to federal advisory boards before their terms had expired. This breach of goodwill is unlikely to be restored. Future transition and beachhead teams should prepare to facilitate such action in turn.[4]

The Biden administration's Department of Justice appeared to be particularly willing to agree to vacate recently promulgated regulations in litigation, rather than simply agree to a remand but leave the existing rule in place while a new regulation was developed. Historically, this practice was resisted unless the district court had decided on the merits that the regulations were unlawful. It is a strategy that can save political appointees the time and effort of going through the administrative notice-and-comment process and interagency review, making it an efficient means to achieve policy goals. Given that the Department of Justice has demonstrated a willingness to take this position, future agency beachhead teams should consider working with the DOJ to resolve such litigation challenges through vacatur in order to realign regulations with a new administration's goals without going through the APA notice-and-comment process.

To help advance their policy agenda more quickly, a new administration's beachhead team should be prepared to work closely with

Congress (depending on its alignment) to apply the Congressional Review Act. This action can save a new administration thousands of hours in changing the regulatory paradigm. The Trump administration was incredibly effective in collaborating with Congress to use this important legal tool.

Finally, newly installed cabinet heads and beachhead teams need to recognize that they will likely be running their respective departments with many appointees not yet confirmed by the Senate for much of the presidential term. Therefore a great deal of care should be taken in positioning capable individuals to exercise the authority of those officials in their absence.

Facilitating Presidential Selection of Agency Staff

Because all four thousand political appointees in the executive branch serve at the pleasure of the president, he has carte blanche in their selection. As a practical matter, this effort is mostly handled by the White House Presidential Personnel Office in coordination with various other White House offices. Each cabinet agency has a White House liaison who coordinates with the Presidential Personnel Office and the political appointees of each department to facilitate the selection of political staff.

Just as interactions between the president and the cabinet secretary differed greatly between President Trump and President George W. Bush, so did the approaches to policy development and the selection of personnel at Interior. The selection of agency personnel during the Bush administration initially appeared to be one of negotiation between the White House and the cabinet officer or agency head. Over time, the process became more accommodating to the cabinet officer. From the beginning of the Trump administration, however, the personnel process appeared to be extremely deferential to the cabinet officer. In my first meeting with Ryan Zinke after his nomination, he explained to me that President Trump had largely given him a free hand in his personnel hires. I was a bit skeptical that this would actually be the case in practice, but Presidential Personnel, as it turned out, was highly deferential to Secretary Zinke's input. Not all of the individuals he put forward made it through the clearance process, but none of them were rejected out of hand by Presidential Personnel. I was very surprised, in light of my experience in the Bush administration. Toward the end of President Trump's tenure, Presidential Personnel became slightly more aggressive in the placement of individuals in specific positions, but my input was always given weight, whether or not it was ultimately followed.

My experience with the presidential selection of agency staff appears to have been very different from that of my successor, Deb Haaland. In June 2021, I witnessed Haaland explain in a Senate congressional hearing that President Biden had nominated an individual to serve as the leader of the Bureau of Land Management whom Haaland had never met or spoken to. Specifically, she said, "I have not met or spoken with Ms. Stone-Manning. I understand that this is the president's nominee and that she is qualified to do the job that he has asked her to do." Later in the hearing, she explained, "I didn't nominate her—I am here to move the department forward on the president's priorities, and that is what I'm focused on at the moment."[5] I couldn't imagine how frustrated I would have been to hear the president announce a nominee to lead one of Interior's subagencies without having sought my input or allowed me the opportunity to meet with the nominee. But in the end, the selection of each appointee rests with the president.

Political appointees serve at the president's pleasure, and someone who wants to serve in the executive branch of the federal government as a political appointee must be acceptable and accountable to the president. The Presidential Personnel Office and agency leadership must do all they can to ensure that the views of political appointees are not at odds with those of the chief executive concerning the issues in their area of responsibility. Potential appointees likewise have an obligation to look carefully at the issues facing the agency and the responsibilities they will be expected to carry out, and ask themselves if their vision lines up with that of the president. Any prospective political appointee can watch the president's campaign speeches and read his policy statements (as well as those of the prospective agency head) to see if their policy positions align. If not, that person should not waste time trying to work in an environment where they do not agree with the policy vision of their boss. I have been stunned that people would seek political appointments knowing full well that their views don't align with the president's, hoping that this divergence would not be noticed by Presidential Personnel. Such self-serving actions can cause needless conflicts and hinder the president's policies.

Learning and Understanding One's Authority

To be effective in the job, political appointees need to understand the statutory or regulatory grants of authority to the position in which they serve, as well as each delegation of authority from superiors to that position. They must also understand what authority their predecessors have delegated to their own subordinates. They need to recognize that they can withdraw such delegations, and should be prepared to do so when appropriate. Understanding the scope of an appointee's authority is essential to driving change successfully within executive agencies.

For a variety of reasons, political leaders sometimes find it convenient to claim that their hands are tied and point to a lower-level official to make a decision. When I served as solicitor, some of my superiors appreciated nothing more than my finding a way to explain that their discretion was limited by the law. They absolutely hated being told they had the freedom to make the policy choice they wanted. It was unbelievable. In my opinion, political appointees' unwillingness to make decisions, despite the fact that Congress tasked them to carry out the law, has created a perception that the decisions made by career staff are somehow more authoritative than decisions rendered by an actual officer of the United States. Such a view negates the very reason for elections: to ensure that executive decisions are the responsibility of individuals who are accountable to the American people.

In addition to understanding their authority for any potential decision or contemplated action, appointees must determine the factors that will serve as the basis of a decision. Some decisions are based entirely on the facts of a situation, some are based entirely on the relevant law, and others are strictly a matter of policy discretion. Many involve all three components. To understand their options in a particular case, appointees must know what sphere they are working in and how much flexibility the law or the policy allows in responding to the factual circumstances. When I was confronted with a difficult question at the Department of the Interior, I often began by laying out a Venn diagram. In one circle were the points of law applicable to the decision. In another were the relevant material facts. In the third circle I would put the recognized policy preference of the president or the secretary. With these issue elements in front of me, I would analyze how they intersected and make sure that the conclusion I reached was rationally connected to the relevant basis for the decision.

Appointees must also understand how the processes of their agency or department normally work. An appointee who deviates from the usual processes must be able to articulate a reason it made sense in a particular case. Those departures from norms will precipitate inquiries—whether legal, congressional, or in the media—so the appointee needs to be able to justify the choice.

Once they have determined that they have the authority to act, understand their decision space, and know the appropriate processes, it is often helpful for appointees to sit down with the senior career staff to clarify the decision space and learn what considerations may have been overlooked. By taking responsibility for a decision—and any associated fallout—a policymaker can defuse controversy and relieve career staff from bearing the brunt of public criticism. When I was working with the National Park Service's cadre of public health officials on our Covid-19 response, for example, I relied on their expertise but made final decisions myself, taking the responsibility of being wrong or right squarely on my shoulders.

Leading Change

When a political appointee who has line authority has received a clear policy vision from the president or agency head, driving change comes down to effort and knowhow. Effort coupled with competence is the biggest factor in success. You don't make change happen simply by telling someone else to do something. If you have the authority, are willing to be consistent, learn what your decision space is, and then have the fortitude to complete what you initiate, you can generally accomplish your objectives as an appointee. But the policy objectives—whether your own or your superior's—need to be clearly articulated to your political team. At the most basic level, communication on priorities is critical so that appointees know what projects should be the main focus of attention in their limited time.

Whenever I stepped into a command situation, I tried to set out my policy expectations clearly to all employees. When I entered the Department of the Interior to serve as deputy secretary, I laid out my expectations to the entire department, consistent with the priorities of Secretary Zinke. When I was sworn in as secretary, I laid out my policy vision and goals in a lengthy email to all employees. (See the

Appendices.) I have always believed it is important to communicate with the career staff from day one—not just setting out your own expectations but also learning as much as you can from them.

I was very fortunate when I rejoined Interior as deputy secretary because my perspective on the effort and processes necessary to drive change had been formed as a staffer in the Bush administration. At the time, I was involved in a lot of department coordination with the secretary and the deputy secretary, both of whom worked long hours with incredible dedication to their mission. I learned a great deal from working with senior leaders every day—reviewing their decision-making materials, witnessing their engagement in team decisions, and seeing how their decisions played out over time.

By having the chance to serve three different Interior secretaries over the course of a decade, I was also able to observe their different approaches to making decisions and the effectiveness of their strategies for implementing policy. I gleaned valuable lessons from each of them before I became the department secretary myself. One of my biggest takeaways was to read everything yourself—don't trust what you are told without verifying it. If, as a reviewer, you believe a document is subpar, it is almost certainly subpar. I never hesitated to modify a document once I carried out a review, not only because that was my duty, but also because the likelihood that anyone else had thoughtfully reviewed the document was quite small. The second main takeaway was that the policymaker needs to be willing to set and stick to deadlines. Nothing will get done in an agency without a deadline. As a leader, you need to be sure that the deadlines are met, even if that means you have to carry out the task yourself. Third, always be willing to listen to constructive criticism from the career team, and make it clear that you value their input. You don't have to accept their ideas, but it is important to give them an opportunity to be heard, so the decisions you ultimately make will be better informed. Finally, you should anticipate running into bumps along the road in driving a policy initiative and be prepared to muster the will to push through obstacles.

As a staffer who was expected to move projects forward, I always believed it was imperative to recognize that the process you choose can make a fundamental difference in your success, particularly with projects that involve many career staff. My efforts to manage projects were most successful when I had: 1) carefully examined my authority; 2) recognized the open questions that needed to be resolved; 3) developed what I thought would be a reasonable process and timeline; and 4) sat down with my senior staff and career Senior Executive Service members to refine the process and set it in motion. The staff knew that I wanted their input but would reserve decisions for myself. They were confident that their views would be considered in the interest of moving the project forward. When career staff were given the opportunity to facilitate a process, they were less likely to be hostile to the project even if they disagreed with the policy goal.

When I served as the solicitor for Interior, I had to address numerous legal questions that would lead to legal opinions on controversial subjects. In doing so, I allowed time for the career attorneys in the office to express their views, so the process was robust even if some advocates outside the department viewed the resulting opinions as controversial. After I left Interior and returned to private practice, I was informed that career lawyers in the office had encouraged my successor to use caution before revoking those legal opinions because they had been crafted with great care and deliberation.

Supporting Your Superiors

Appointees must try to provide their superiors with unbiased, intellectually honest advice regarding their options under the law. The president's preferred policy outcomes can usually be achieved in various ways, but in the unlikely event that Congress has not delegated authority to the agency to take the president's preferred action, political appointees should make that fact clear to their superiors and suggest how such authority could be gained. Each position I held in the executive branch required me to examine my authority and think about how I might help my superiors succeed—whether political appointees or the president himself. When I was a young staffer, that often meant accepting public responsibility for the errors of more senior political appointees so they didn't need to take the heat. At other times, it meant being creative to accomplish the administration's goals.

For example, from the outset of the Trump administration, one primary focus of Interior was increasing opportunities for recreational activities and improving the condition of the facilities in our national parks, to provide a concrete success for the president's conservation stewardship vision. As part of this project, we dramatically expanded public access to lands managed by the Department of the Interior. One of our initiatives was the development and enactment of legislation that would provide funding to tackle the National Park Service's deferred maintenance backlog and permanently authorize funding for the department's Land and Water Conservation Fund, established to protect natural areas and support recreational opportunities. But the effort to develop the legislation and gather support in Congress for its passage was going nowhere when I took the helm of the department.

Similar proposals had languished for decades, so I knew I had to think outside the box to get any legislation passed. We needed to devise a plan to build momentum in the Senate and garner public support for the effort. I approached the White House and arranged visits to our national parks by Vice President Mike Pence, Karen Pence, Melania Trump, and Ivanka Trump. These visits drew media attention to the need for better maintenance of our parks (which

Congress had to address), fostered a positive view of the legislative proposal in the White House, and gave the public a window into the administration's priorities. As soon as we gained the president's backing for the legislation, I pressed the issue on the Hill to secure bipartisan support. The enactment of what became known as the Great American Outdoors Act will eventually be viewed as one of the most consequential funding bills in history for recreational opportunities and improved facilities on our nation's public lands.

Just as political appointees should think creatively to support their superiors, so should they aim to ensure that younger team members have a chance to learn from the current leadership team. After all, these team members will be the most likely candidates to serve in future administrations. To that end, the agency leadership should make an effort to cultivate a strong sense of camaraderie and shared perspective by having regular all-political meetings, ensuring that everyone on the team understands the administration's goals and recognizes the limited amount of time they have to accomplish policy objectives. In truth, I learned as much from the setbacks of my superiors as from their successes, and I don't doubt that my tenure as a department head provided similar lessons to the next generation of Interior appointees.

"Has the Secretary Fired You Yet?"

One of the most memorable ad hoc lessons I received on support-ing one's superiors came about when I was leading the Office of Congressional and Legislative Affairs at Interior. I was summoned to the hideaway office of Senator Ted Stevens of Alaska, who held a hugely important position as chair of the Senate Appropria-tions Committee. Since Interior has a very large responsibility in Alaska, there is always a relationship between the department and the Alaska Senate offices. Senator Stevens had previously served as a political appointee at Interior and then as the U.S. attorney in Alaska.

In his hideaway office, Stevens told me that he was unhappy with a policy position that Secretary Norton was taking on an issue. He looked at me and asked, "Have you been fired by the secretary yet?"

"Of course not," I replied, more than a little puzzled.

"In that case," he said, "you must not be doing your job."

In the face of my confusion, Stevens explained that if I were doing my job I would have driven home the problem with Norton's policy position until she decided to fire me. He further said that he had been "fired" multiple times while serving as legislative counsel at Interior. (I assumed that he was being hyperbolic.)

His point was elegant and simple: everybody wants to bring good news to their superior, but it's more important as a political appointee to convey the facts, whether or not the secretary wants to hear them. The secretary is free to ignore your views, but you owe them your honest assessment. That guidance was extremely valuable to me. The lesson was clear: don't ever be afraid to share your perspective with a decision maker, regardless of what the consequences might be. As a political appointee, you owe your input to your superior, who expects to receive your best advice.

Asking Questions and Providing Accurate Information

As a young appointee, I asked a lot of questions of everyone I met with in the agency. I made an effort to read the subject matter before every meeting so I could understand the factual and legal setting for a decision. In many cases it was clear that the manager responsible for a project had not even read the briefing documents that staff members had compiled. As a result, questions posed to the manager could become awkward. At the end of the Bush administration, a senior career executive came into my office to say goodbye and mentioned that he couldn't believe how fearless I was in asking questions. I thought it a bizarre statement. In my eight-year tenure, I had never contemplated the possibility that there was a downside to asking a question, and over time my approach enabled me to identify flawed decisions before they were rubber-stamped by other political appointees. Asking questions increased my knowledge of department policies so I could better support my superiors and the White House. It built up my understanding of the facts and the law so I could speak with confidence to my superiors.

While I was serving as the director of congressional and legislative affairs, I was invited to attend a meeting with the other agency congressional affairs directors about the White House's expectations for calls with political appointees. It was an enlightening discussion. A high-level White House staffer explained that if the White House called an agency appointee, the appointee needed to remember that they worked for the president first and foremost. If an appointee provided incorrect information to the White House, they could expect to leave their position. At first the policy seemed harsh, but the rationale was that there were only a certain number of days in a presidential term and the White House did not have the time to double-check an appointee's work. When the policy was explained, it sounded reasonable to me. If the White House cannot trust you to provide accurate information, you will be asked to leave, so double-check your work before you convey information up the ladder. It needs to be correct.

Knowing Whether You Have the Ball, Watching the Clock, and Avoiding Delays

One of my biggest accountability lessons in Washington followed the loss of a legislative initiative. I had been told by other members of the political team that they were on top of the issue and I didn't need to worry about it, even though it fell within my area of responsibility. When the legislative setback occurred, the White House and the secretary were looking at one person—me. After that incident, I never forgot the lesson: while every victory has a thousand fathers, a defeat shows everyone exactly who was accountable.

As a political appointee, you can't assume that any assistance you get on a project will be useful. You should expect that you will often be given incomplete or inaccurate information when you make an inquiry of the career staff, as illustrated by the incidents recorded in the work of James Sherk and highlighted in Chapter 2. In some cases, the failing may seem malicious. If you sense that a detail is not supported, you must insist on going through the facts yourself. As a corollary, you must be sure that a project's timeline allows for addressing problems with the work product done by staff.

I learned that lesson the hard way early in my first job at Interior. The chief of staff to the secretary assigned me a project that had already been delegated to someone in the office of an assistant secretary. When I went to my colleague to check the status of the project, he made it clear that I would receive it at a time that would allow me only a very short window to review and clear the document. Then, he was a couple of days late in sending me the product, and it was a disaster. I thought maybe I could salvage the document by working all night and turn it in a few hours late, but I would need assistance. No one was available at the office to work overnight, so I called my wife, Gena, and begged her to come in to help with inputting the changes while I reworked the product. We finished a revised draft by morning, but it was quite an unpleasant experience. Gena informed me in no uncertain terms that she would not be coming in to save the day ever again.

My expectation that I would receive a good product from a teammate was flawed. I should have insisted on seeing the document earlier or taking over the project the minute it appeared likely to be late. Without my review, the product would have been an embarrassing document submitted under the secretary's name, but my willingness to wait for it had taken time away from the White House reviewer. My key takeaway was: always give a deadline and stay on top of people between deadlines to keep the political appointee from getting in trouble. In times when some career staff are in open resistance mode, as during the Trump administration, it is especially important to bird-dog projects in order to avoid negligence or sabotage.

A presidential term is 1,461 days. In the absence of a second term, everything that is not accomplished by day 1,461 is probably never going to be done. Every day that progress is not made on an administration's priorities is a day the administration won't get back. It is therefore imperative for political appointees to develop a conceptual timeline for each priority, including every ordinary review process that will be needed to get to a final outcome. In many cases, various reviews take place in the agency's internal offices. The appointee needs to identify what those processes are and how long they may take, as well as determining whether those processes can be bypassed and who authorizes such an action. In other cases, multiple agencies and executive offices, such as the Office of Management and Budget, are involved in the review process. These agencies may set their own priorities independently, which can greatly affect a review timeline. For example, in the latter half of the Trump administration, the OMB's Office of Information and Regulatory Affairs chose to slow down a number of proposed regulations from Interior that were undergoing review. Numerous regulatory packages were therefore never finalized.

After you have set a timeline, you must do everything in your power to keep it. That means staying on top of those tasked with developing the product, and intervening to get it done if they are not making progress. At times, it also means elevating an issue up for resolution. If a resolution cannot be achieved, the superior must determine that the priority is no longer a priority. On the flip side, once an issue is resolved, the appointee may then need to work overtime to bring the progress back on schedule.

Collaborating with White House Staff

Whether the president engages with a cabinet secretary directly or through staff, political appointees at all levels can expect to get a variety of calls from White House staff: seeking information, asking for the development of policy recommendations, or even requesting that a particular action be taken on a certain matter. A political appointee must take care not to drag the White House into controversy by improper handling of an inquiry or demand. My practice as a staffer, at any level, was first to determine the propriety of the request, and then quickly get the appropriate clearance from the secretary's office before proceeding. I tried to remember that the White House staffer was working on an urgent timeline, but proceeding before the department's leadership thought through the action could have terrible consequences. For example, there are many situations where the mere appearance of White House involvement in a decision could lead to many questions from Congress, the public, the inspector general, and the FBI. In every position I held, I always believed it was important that the secretary's office be made aware of the contact with White House staff. If a new policy discussion is occurring at the White House, for example, the secretary's office may have a particular view on who should attend that policy development meeting.

As a rule, I avoided creating a situation where White House staff engaged directly with a career employee, which could lead to misunderstanding, on both sides, of where decision-making authority resides and what are the protocols for making a decision. When a White House staffer demanded to speak with a particular agency employee, I first talked to the employee myself and explained that person's role and my own as a political appointee. With the secretary's approval, I met with the White House staff and the career staffer jointly, again clarifying the ground rules regarding everyone's roles and authority. Agency decisions are made by agency officials, not White House political staffers. The White House staff are committed to achieving the president's agenda, but often are unaware of protocols or procedures within the agency. Their zeal to take action could therefore end up harming the president. An agency appointee needs to understand the request from the White House, elevate it, and let the secretary's office figure out how to approach it.

"It's Too Complicated for Congress," So Don't Count on It to Bail You Out

One of the more disheartening days of my public service occurred during the Bush administration, right after a congressional hearing. Senator Daniel Inouye of Hawaii (D), whom I had greatly admired for decades, approached me about the subject of the hearing. "David," he said, "this issue was too complicated for Congress to deal with."

As I stood in one of the most majestic hearing rooms in the Senate, I looked at him and said, "Congress is who is supposed to make complicated policy decisions. I understand that Congress may not want to work on an issue, but Senator, this branch of government is precisely where the Framers thought these issues would be resolved."

He patted my arm, acknowledged that Congress really should act, and gently conveyed that it was not going to happen until the political need to act was more acute. It was a wonderful lesson in the reality of legislative priorities.

When the stakes are extraordinarily high, such as during the 2008 financial crisis or the Covid-19 pandemic, Congress can move with lightning speed. But the stakes are rarely that high, and few members of Congress regularly engage in any activity that builds the consensus needed to modify the status quo in a significant way. Instead, congressional activity is often largely focused on incrementally adding to existing government programs that already have a broad base of entrenched political support.

Ideally, agency leaders work hard to cultivate positive relations with the members of Congress who serve on their agency's authorizing and appropriations committees. That can be a challenge in today's highly partisan environment, but communicating regularly with lawmakers allows agency heads to seize on legislative opportunities to drive the administration's priorities forward. Legislative success is likely to be far more durable than a regulatory initiative. Most political appointees in the executive branch will interact with Congress in a variety of ways, and these interactions are important. Officials of the executive branch have an interest in protecting its prerogatives, but the vast majority of issues between the branches can be addressed through accommodation. I usually found that a visit with a member of Congress from either side of the aisle would inure to my benefit at some later point. When specific members of Congress were difficult to deal with, I tried to remember that they were elected by their constituency. They had earned the right to act in the manner they thought best for their constituents, and it was their voters, not some political appointee, who would judge their performance and ultimately determine their success in office.

Dealing with Difficult Staff

I was at an airport in early 2018 when I read a stomach-churning draft report from the Office of Inspector General on the reassignment of Senior Executive Service (SES) members at Interior the previous spring, before my return to the department. I turned to my wife, who has served as a career civil servant for nearly three decades, and told her about the findings, which prompted a major shake of her head.

The draft report painted an unflattering picture of how the Trump administration appointees at the Department of the Interior had conducted the lawful reassignment of nearly three dozen Senior Executive Service employees within the department. According to the report, the new administration "did not document its plan or the reasons it used when selecting senior executives for reassignment, nor did it gather the information needed to make informed decisions about the reassignments."[6] Consequently, the affected employees "questioned whether these reassignments were political or punitive, based on a prior conflict with DOI leadership, or on the senior executive's nearness to retirement."

In itself, the new political leadership's decision to reassign career Senior Executive Service members was lawful, appropriate, and important. A new administration refocuses policy priorities and begins to assign members of the SES to positions where the leadership believes they will best serve the organization and advance the administration's priorities. Reassignment decisions cannot be made from improper motivations such as political affiliation. That had not happened in this case, but there were understandable questions about procedure.

When the Senior Executive Service was established in 1978, its purpose was to "ensure that the executive management of the Government of the United States is responsive to the needs, policies, and goals of the nation."[7] The law provides, among other things, that federal agencies have the authority to assign executives where they will be most effective in accomplishing the agency's mission and where the best use will be made of their talents. At the same time, SES employees are to be protected from arbitrary actions and unlawful personnel practices. Within each agency, the management of the SES is done through the Executive Resources Board (ERB) on behalf of the secretary.

In September 2009, the Office of Personnel Management developed best-practice guidelines for ERBs, yet no effort had been made to adopt and implement these guidelines at the Department of the Interior between then and January 2017. At the beginning of the Trump administration, career staff either were unaware of these recommendations or failed to inform the new political team of their existence. In carrying out the reassignments that the Trump administration wanted done, the ERB did not follow those best-practice guidelines—which had never been implemented during the Obama administration. In addition, the career staff in the department and its agencies did a poor job of documenting their justifications for the reassignments, and the political leadership failed to scrutinize the documents carefully.

While the legal requirements for the reassignments were met, the process of reassigning the employees was far below the best practices. Reading the draft report, I couldn't help but think it would do unnecessary damage to the image of the new administration both inside and outside the government. It would not be widely known that Obama administration appointees at Interior had never adopted the recommended best practices, nor would anyone care that the career staff had not informed the new appointees about those optimal processes. The appointees, for their part, had not asked the necessary questions to ascertain best practices and ensure that they were followed and properly documented. They had made decisions based on what they understood to be correct and expected their staff to handle each case appropriately, rather than fly-specking their actions. These assumptions were wrong.

One takeaway for me was that political appointees need to ask a lot of questions, about processes as well as substance, not just assume that their subordinates will properly and effectively implement their directives, or that career staff will alert the political leadership of the consequences that might result from carrying out a flawed directive. Career staff can do damage to an administration's agenda by simply not doing their own jobs well. Political appointees should always seek to understand the best practices for a particular situation before taking action. They can choose to depart from a best practice, but at the risk of drawing criticism of the underlying decision itself. In that event, they should be prepared to explain their rationale to Congress and the public. Making the effort to learn the agency's processes and best practices at the outset can go a long way toward mitigating the potential risks associated with driving an administration's agenda forward.

While most staff in an agency want to be helpful and take direction, many do not. It is important that staff clearly understand a political appointee's authority. When a junior appointee encounters a staffer who is part of a resistance effort, however, the appointee should not engage in a confrontation, but instead work with the supervisor to find an appropriate solution. At times, human resources and agency lawyers are needed to handle the situation. Political appointees have tools for dealing with staff who will not perform their job functions. Many behavioral problems can be shut down so that a project will succeed, but this involves time and diligence.

Taking the Weaponization of FOIA and IGs in Stride

As we saw earlier, laws have been enacted to place transparency requirements on the executive branch and establish investigative processes for possible misconduct—particularly the Freedom of Information Act and the Inspector General Act. It is important for executive agency employees and political appointees to recognize that these processes will be leveraged by partisans and activists to attack your credibility, your ethical compliance, and the soundness of your decisions. At times, lawmakers will call for investigations before the relevant decisions are made by an agency. In 2008, for example, Secretary Kempthorne was working diligently to make a decision about the listing of the polar bear as an endangered species, but it was taking time due to various deliberations within the department and across the administration. Senator Barbara Boxer of California demanded an investigation into the delay, and the inspector general decided to start the investigation before a decision was made. In fact, I was being interviewed by the investigators when Secretary Kempthorne's office called and asked me to come down to discuss the polar bear question.

Equally concerning, the investigators in the inspector general's office frequently operate with little oversight. They have their own biases and can produce extremely flawed work. In my experience, the press won't highlight any flaws in the published report, but only the subjective conclusions. This is also the case with reports from Congress. Thus, it's important for prospective political appointees to understand the reputational risk posed by the inspector general (even when their superiors disagree with the investigation's conclusions) before signing up for public service.

Likewise, political appointees need to recognize that virtually anything they say or write is likely to be documented and eventually disclosed through the Freedom of Information Act or through congressional oversight. Appointees must realize that there is no such thing as confidential communication in the government, and they must strive to ensure that their communications are always deliberate and measured, in every situation. The lack of confidentiality must never lead to unwillingness to inquire or explain, but it's imperative that political appointees do so in a manner that they and their superiors will not later regret.

Navigating Day One as a Political Appointee

The first day or two as a political appointee can be a bit chaotic. The first and most important thing an appointee does is take the oath of office. It is the same for everyone:

> I, [NAME], do solemnly swear (or affirm) that I will support and defend the Constitution of the United States against all enemies, foreign and domestic; that I will bear true faith and allegiance to the same; that I take this obligation freely, without any mental reservation or purpose of evasion; and that I will well and faithfully discharge the duties of the office on which I am about to enter. So help me God.

The commitment to support and defend the Constitution of the United States and "well and faithfully discharge the duties of the office on which I am about to enter" has carried great weight with me every time I've taken the oath. While the first clause is easy to view as the most important, I believe that the obligations in the latter clause are equally immense. The duties of a particular office are often not fully clear when the oath is taken, but the employee's sworn obligation is to carry out the responsibilities of the job "well and faithfully." My experiences in my varied appointments have convinced me that political appointees must strive to approach each decision and action with an open mind, seek input from others, and listen to a variety of perspectives to ensure that their recommendations and conclusions are sufficiently well informed to meet the standard of fulfilling responsibilities "well and faithfully."

On the first day, appointees receive their position description, or "PD," which they need to review with their supervisor to clarify expectations. Often, the expectations of the supervisor are about as clear as mud. In the first week, there are normally several briefings that are very important for new political appointees, though not always taken seriously. These briefings include information about federal ethics regulations, the Freedom of Information Act, the Federal Records Act, and data security. A failure to understand and meet the requirements of these laws can have disastrous consequences.

Criticisms about legal compliance are routinely leveled against political appointees both by nongovernmental organizations and by elected officials of the other party, since the easiest way to take the steam out of an initiative is to mire it in controversy. The allegations are often run by the press with little concern for the facts. The problem often comes down to whether the political appointee established a culture of compliance in their office or simply expected others to figure out what is required. If the inspector general highlights an issue, political appointees should not expect someone else to be watching their back. The best way of protecting themselves and the administration is to become familiar with the rules, seeking counsel when they are unclear, and then adhere to them. This is particularly important in the case of a policy decision that is weighty or likely to be controversial.

Every political appointee with operational responsibility needs to make an effort to understand precisely how decisions flow within their organization, in the executive branch writ large, and out to the public. There are a multitude of "paper flow" processes, and political appointees should understand these processes and ensure informed participation in them, so that the administration's priorities are accurately reflected in any comments that are provided to the Executive Office of the President or to other federal agencies.

Political appointees entering an administration must be prepared to let go of any preconceived expectations of their roles, unless they are leading the organization. The decision to join an administration and work in a federal agency constitutes a leap of faith, especially if you have never done so before. You have no idea what you are in for, and everything can change on a dime. The unexpected can happen any day.

During the interview process for my very first job at the Department of the Interior, I explained that I would do any job to help the secretary except one: running the Office of Congressional and Legislative Affairs. A few weeks after I entered government service, the secretary's chief of staff pulled me into a meeting and explained that my duties were going to change. I would keep my current title, but they were adding another job to my responsibilities. The chief of staff proceeded to inform me that the additional responsibilities were those of the one job I had said I wouldn't do: leading the Office of Congressional and Legislative Affairs. After I left his office, I thought it through and decided that I had joined the administration to help make a difference, and if people thought I was needed in that particular position, I would strive to do my best work. I served in that job for nearly four years, then was quickly elevated over the next four years largely based on my performance and the secretary's needs. During the Trump administration, I occasionally had the responsibility of explaining to appointees that the department had a need I thought they could fill. I suspected that they most likely didn't want that job, and I knew precisely how they felt!

Improving the Agency You Serve

I believe that political appointees should endeavor to leave their organization functioning better than they found it. During my tenure as solicitor, I invested a great deal of time in improving the Interior Department's technological capacity and developing basic business practices so attorneys could better document their work. During my second tour in the department, beyond the president's agenda on conservation stewardship, recreation, and energy independence, I focused much effort on ensuring that the ethics office implemented enhanced best practices to create a culture of ethical compliance, and also on modernizing the processing of FOIA requests. In my view, when political appointees have the opportunity to lead, they should strive to accomplish meaningful change in the agency, to increase efficiency and provide better service to the American people.

I always sought input from employees on ways to improve the organization. As deputy secretary, I set up an electronic ideas box for staff input. As secretary, I regularly sought feedback from staff in the field. Both of these approaches provided many suggestions for improving the department. For example, we waived park entrance fees for veterans and Gold Star family members, an idea proposed by a staff member during a visit to Indiana Dunes National Park. We also implemented a staff member's idea for improving the National Environmental Policy Act's review process by including timeframes and page limits for documents. Occasionally, I had staff tell me that their own career leadership had advised them not to suggest improvements because their colleagues in the National Park Service would not take kindly to it and their future in the agency would be grim. I was astonished that an organizational culture would be so hostile to thinking about how things could be done better, but that was the prevailing culture in pockets of the National Park Service.

Taking the Opportunity to Serve

The nation needs competent, experienced administrators to serve at both career and political levels of the federal executive branch. Today's rancorous political environment makes these responsibilities less and less appealing. On the other hand, the American people deserve a government that serves them better. When I decided to return for a second tour of duty at the Department of the Interior, I knew every potential downside to myself and my family that would likely come from leaving our comfortable private life to serve in government, but I nonetheless stepped forward. I believe the nation is in great need of people who will step forward and work to address the many challenges we face. If you believe in the goodness of the American people, and in the need for government at any level to better serve the public, do not hesitate to step forward and make an effort to improve your community, your state, or your country. Just do not ever forget that you report to them and the president.

CONCLUSION

Virtually every day, the headlines are filled with demonstrable failures of the administrative state. Only a short while ago it was unimaginable that our nation would face a shortage of baby formula exacerbated by bureaucratic delay, or witness a massive embarrassment of flawed military and diplomatic action such as the withdrawal from Afghanistan. Our leaders and our institutions are failing the American people, despite the massive expansion of these institutions.

The preceding pages have highlighted the tremendous growth of the federal government and the creeping concentration of power in administrative agencies, where much of that power has been handed to a career civil service that is increasingly distant from political accountability. American citizens' voice in representative government has diminished as the power of those they elect to represent them is ceded to functionally unaccountable agency staff. Unfortunately, many of these agency employees tend to align with the ideology of one political party and work to "resist" the other.

Members of Congress from both parties have found it politically beneficial to punt significant questions of public policy to a federal workforce that cannot be voted out. These unelected agency actors wield their delegated power with little political oversight. Americans have seen their constitutional rights encroached upon by flawed agency enforcement and adjudication systems. Doctrines of judicial deference to agency decisions have encouraged aggressive action by the executive branch. The American people deserve better from those who seek elective office in Congress, and from those who choose to serve in the executive branch or the judiciary.

The Founders' vision of a nation governed by the consent of the governed is waning, and the people's voice in representative government grows weaker as administrative agencies gain more power. But this doesn't have to continue. The solution is as simple as the swamp of administrative agencies is complex: everyone in public office must seriously reflect on their oath and start doing their job as it was designed.

The American people must demand that the president, members of Congress, judges, political appointees, and career agency staff strive to fulfill the obligations of their roles according to their proper authority—neither evading responsibility nor exercising unauthorized power. The president must embrace his duty as the chief executive to see that the nation's laws are faithfully executed, and should be aggressive in demanding that agencies provide better results for the American people. The president has a robust toolkit of oversight options that he can harness to rein in rogue agency actors, such as the removal power and regulatory review authority. Agency leaders must drive the president's preferred policies forward as their authority permits, or seek to secure legislative authorization from Congress if needed. Agency leaders must do the hard work of overseeing staff and holding poor performers to account. A political appointee who does not seek to drive change fails both the president and the electorate.

But the buck doesn't stop with elected representatives and political appointees. Career agency staff must return to the first principles of public service and support the vision of the people's chosen chief executive. Efforts to resist or derail the policy preferences of the elected president in favor of personal or institutional biases also undermine representative government. Unchecked attempts by agency staff to lay claim to power above and beyond what Congress has delegated to the agency exacerbate the failure of accountability. Agency staff must understand the laws they are tasked with administering and not seek to exercise power beyond their purview without securing congressional authorization. They are not in government to be policy zealots untethered by law.

I believe that the blueprint for accountable government already exists. It is found in the Constitution's separation of powers and in the oath taken by every career civil servant, every executive appointee, every member of Congress, and every federal judge. They each must start doing their respective jobs "well and faithfully." They report to you and me.

APPENDICES

1 – Department of the Interior Organizational Chart

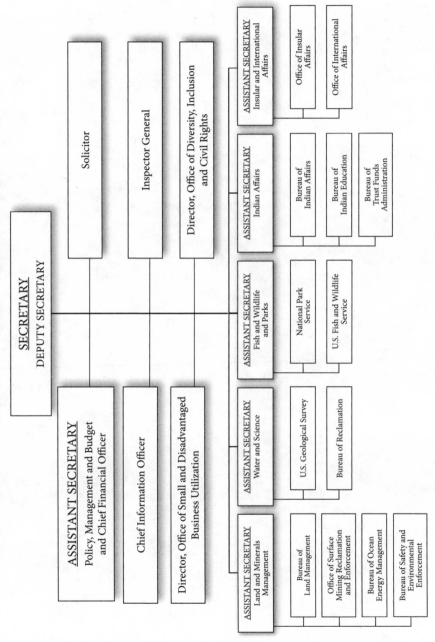

2 – DAY ONE SECRETARIAL ORDER IMPLEMENTING PRESIDENT TRUMP'S AGENDA

Order No. 3347
Subject: Conservation Stewardship and Outdoor Recreation

SEC. 1 – PURPOSE
The Department of the Interior (Department) is entrusted with overseeing Federal lands for the benefit of current and future generations. This includes advancing conservation stewardship and increasing outdoor recreation opportunities, including hunting and fishing, for all Americans. The purpose of this Order is to enhance conservation stewardship, increase outdoor recreation, and improve the management of game species and their habitat.

SEC. 2 – BACKGROUND
Led by recreational hunters and anglers, America's conservation and outdoor recreation movements continue to be led by individual sportsmen working together with ranchers, farmers, state wildlife agencies, non-profit sportsmen-conservation organizations, and the Department.

The Department has vast management responsibilities across our Nation's Federal lands, waters, and mineral resources. In addition to overseeing with humility the conservation and management of fish and wildlife resources, the Department also stewards 20 percent of the Nation's lands, oversees the responsible development of over 20 percent of U.S. energy supplies, serves as the largest supplier and manager of water in 17 Western States, and maintains relationships with over 500 federally recognized tribes. Over 400 units of the National Park System provide unique outdoor recreation opportunities as well as preserve and protect nearly 27,000 historic structures, more than 700 landscapes, and nearly 100,000 archaeological properties. The Department has also partnered with over 45,000 landowners and 3,000 conservation partners to restore successfully more than one million acres of wetland habitat, three million acres of upland habitat, and 11,000 miles of streams.

President Theodore Roosevelt loved the outdoors, vigorously hunted wildlife, and developed a uniquely American conservation ethos. Executive Order 13443 built on President Roosevelt's conservation legacy and directed Federal agencies, including the Department of the Interior, to facilitate the expansion and enhancement of hunting opportunities and management of game species and their habitat.

As a servant of the American people, the Department will continue to strengthen President Roosevelt's conservation stewardship legacy through this Order by seeking to expand recreational and conservation opportunities for all Americans.

SEC. 3 – AUTHORITY

This Order is issued under the authority of Section 2 of Reorganization Plan No. 3 of 1950 (64 Stat. 1262), as amended, as well as the Department's land and resource management authorities, including the following:

- Fish and Wildlife Act of 1956, as amended, 16 U.S.C. 742a, et seq.;
- National Wildlife Refuge System Improvement Act of 1997, as amended, 16 U.S.C. 668dd et seq.;
- Federal Land Policy and Management Act of 1976, as amended, 43 U.S.C. 1701, et seq.;
- National Park Service Organic Act of 1916, as amended, 54 U.S.C. 100101, et seq.; and

- Executive Order 13443, "Facilitation of Hunting Heritage and Wildlife Conservation."

SEC. 4 – CONSERVATION STEWARDSHIP AND OUTDOOR
RECREATION DIRECTIVE

 A. This Order directs the Assistant Secretary for Fish and Wildlife and Parks and the Assistant Secretary for Land and Minerals Management to:

  (1) Report to the Secretary within 30 calendar days on:

   a. All actions taken to implement Executive Order 13443 and achieve its goals.

   b. All actions described in Executive Order 13443 that have not occurred, along with an explanation of any regulatory, legislative, policy or other barriers that have prevented or slowed successful implementation of Executive Order 13443.

   c. Specific recommendations to improve implementation of Executive Order 13443.

  (2) Report to the Secretary within 30 calendar days with specific recommendations to enhance recreational fishing, specifically regarding efforts to enhance and expand recreational fishing access.

 B. Upon approval of the reports by the Secretary, the Department shall:

  (1) Submit the first report to the Wildlife and Hunting Heritage Conservation Council (WHHCC) with a request for the WHHCC's consensus recommendations for improving implementation of Executive Order 13443.

  (2) Submit the second report to the Sport Fishing and Boating Partnership Council (SFBPC) with a request for the SFBPC's consensus recommendations for enhancing and expanding recreational fishing access.

C. Once WHHCC and SFBPC have responded with recommendations, the Department shall, within 30 calendar days:

    (1) Identify specific actions to expand access significantly for recreational hunting and fishing on public lands as may be appropriate.

    (2) Identify specific actions to improve recreational hunting and fishing cooperation, consultation, and communication with state wildlife managers.

    (3) Identify specific actions to improve habitat for fish and wildlife.

    (4) Identify specific actions to manage predators effectively and efficiently.

    (5) Encourage, promote, and facilitate greater public access to all Department lands consistent with applicable laws.

D. The Secretary will designate an appointee in the Immediate Office of the Secretary to coordinate all activities by and among the Department, the WHHCC, the SFBPC, and their respective Designated Federal Officers with respect to implementation of this Order.

SEC. 5 – EFFECT OF ORDER

This Order is intended to improve the internal management of the Department. This Order and any resulting reports or recommendations are not intended to, and do not, create any right or benefit, substantive or procedural, enforceable at law or equity by a party against the United States, its departments, agencies, instrumentalities or entities, its officers or employees, or any other person. To the extent there is any inconsistency between the provisions of this Order and any Federal laws or regulations, the laws or regulations will control.

Sec. 6 – Expiration Date

This Order is effective immediately and will remain in effect until it is amended, superseded, or revoked.

Ryan Zinke
Secretary of the Interior
March 2, 2017

3 – Day One All-Employee Message from Deputy Secretary Bernhardt

Good Morning. My name is David Bernhardt. Earlier today, I took the oath of office to serve as the Department of the Interior's Deputy Secretary. I look forward to working with many of you in my capacity as the Deputy Secretary and the Department's chief operating officer.

Many of you have already gotten to know Secretary Zinke over the last several months. So, I will simply say that I am humbled to serve as his right hand as we move forward with his and the President's priorities. I am honored to be a part of a team that is focused on getting things working again. The Secretary recognizes that we are here to serve the American people, and he is committed to leaving Interior in better shape than he found it. So am I.

Some of you are aware that this is my second tour of duty within the Department of the Interior. I previously spent eight years working in the Office of the Secretary and the Office of the Solicitor. As I walked into the Main Interior Office Building this morning many great memories flooded back. In particular, I felt appreciation for the significant lessons I have learned during that first tour from many current, and now retired, employees within the bureaus, the Office of the Secretary, and the Office of the Solicitor.

As a Westerner and Sportsman, my appreciation for the Department's mission is deeply felt. I love its history and the diversity of the bureau's missions. My desire to ensure that its future is bright is unequivocal. My respect for and care of the laws that Congress has provided us to carry out our mission is real. I also believe there are bounds to our authority. To the extent such bounds exist, we should not try to stretch the law like a fraying rubber band to fit a particular policy vision. Instead, we should ask Congress for the authority we want or need—if it's so important for us to have.

As I swore the oath of office, my attention was captured by the final clause which states "that I will well and faithfully discharge the duties of the office on which I am about to enter." Each of you made an identical commitment when joining public service. Promising to carry out one's duties "well and faithfully" is a meaningful commitment. In complete candor, it is possible this clause resonated with me because I have just gone through the Senate confirmation process. Going through a public three-month-long interview and approval process can have a few humbling moments. However, it also crystalizes a few thoughts and teaches a few lessons. I am going to share a few of those with you.

My first thought is that, given the hyperbole of today's public discourse, you and I and everyone else within the Department really are in the soup together. We may not like it. But it is the way it is. This means my conduct will reflect on you. Yours will reflect on me and your other colleagues. All of our conduct reflects on the Secretary.

Second, unfortunately we are living in a world where a few people are not discharging their duties faithfully or well. They have forgotten their oath. Instead, they choose to parrot comments of special interests rather than carry out their governmental duties to move the country forward. By doing so, they often avoid grounding their views in the actual facts or the law. Such conduct is arbitrary. It is lazy. We must always refrain from taking such a path. The decisions we make here have consequences. We must understand the factual setting and our actual decision space. Our conclusions must be connected to the facts that exist, not to the facts or the law that we might wish existed to fit our preferred outcome.

Third, a little kindness when interacting with others can make a big difference to a citizen or a colleague. During my confirmation hearing, before asking me a question, a Senator paused to pay my daughter a kind compliment. While my confirmation hearing was probably not a very big deal to that Senator, it felt like a big deal to my kids. His gesture meant a lot to my family. That gesture reinforced my commitment to strive to treat colleagues and citizens in a manner that I hope others would treat our daughters, sons or partners. Consider doing the same thing. When we interact with others, particularly the public, we represent the weight of the entire government. What may seem like an unimportant interaction to us in any given moment might actually be a pretty big deal to the person we are interacting with. The decisions we make can have great consequence to them, and such small gestures can reap large benefits for everyone involved.

Finally, we can disagree on important issues without being disagreeable. At the same confirmation hearing, a Senator who clearly does not agree with the Administration's policy vision questioned my policy views. He stated his position. He asked me the questions he wanted to ask. He challenged my responses where he disagreed. Although we see things differently, he was not challenging my motivations, my intentions or my morality because of this difference in opinion. I left with respect for him. His actions were precisely what I believe our public policy discourse process should be.

I believe each of us choose to come to the Department because we believe in serving the people. We love the Department's mission. We want to make it even better. We maintain those values even when our conclusions differ. We can have healthy disagreement. However, ultimately, it is the policymaker's job, to the extent they have discretion, to exercise that discretion in accord with the administration's view. This is because each President represents the will of the people, until the next one is sworn in.

In addition to these points, I want to remind you of a few other basic principles of conduct that each of us are bound by. These 14 principles were originally issued by President George H. W. Bush, in an executive order, and they were subsequently issued in the *Standards of Ethical Conduct for Employees of the Executive Branch* at 5 CFR § 2635.101(b). I have slightly modified them for readability, but you can find the originals on the Department's Ethics Office website at https://www.doi.gov/ethics/basic-obligations-of-public-service. Simply put:

1. Public service is a public trust, requiring us to place loyalty to the Constitution, the laws and ethical principles above private gain.
2. I won't hold financial interests that conflict with the conscientious performance of duty.
3. I won't engage in financial transactions using nonpublic Government information or allow the improper use of such information to further any private interest.
4. I won't, except in particular conditions approved by regulations of the ethics office, solicit or accept any gift or other item of monetary value from any person or entity seeking official action from, doing business with, or conducting activities regulated by our agency, or whose interests may be substantially affected by the performance or nonperformance of my duties.
5. I will put forth honest effort in the performance of my duties.
6. I will not make unauthorized commitments or promises of any kind purporting to bind the Government.
7. I will not use public office for private gain.
8. I will act impartially and will not give preferential treatment to any private organization or individual.
9. I will protect and conserve Federal property and shall not use it for other than authorized activities.
10. I will not engage in outside employment or activities, including seeking or negotiating for employment,

that conflict with the official Government duties and responsibilities.

11. I will disclose waste, fraud, abuse, and corruption to the appropriate authorities, which includes reporting to our management or the Inspector General.

12. I will satisfy in good faith my obligations as a citizen, including all just financial obligations, especially those— such as Federal, State, or local taxes—that are imposed by law.

13. I shall adhere to all laws and regulations that provide equal opportunity for all Americans regardless of race, color, religion, sex, national origin, age, sexual orientation or handicap.

14. I will endeavor to avoid any actions creating the appearance that I am violating the law. the Standards of Ethical Conduct for Employees of the Executive Branch, the Department's supplemental ethics regulations, or relevant executive orders. This is most easily facilitated by communicating with the ethics officials within the Department of the Interior, which I will do.

Finally, since the Secretary had a big head start in moving forward with the President's vision, I will spend a few days listening and visiting with you to learn where things stand. To those of you I know, I look forward to catching up. To those of you I don't, I look forward to getting to know you.

Respectfully,
David Bernhardt
Deputy Secretary

4 – Day One All-Employee Message
from Secretary Bernhardt

Colleagues:

It is a privilege to write to you in a new capacity. I was appointed by the President as the Secretary of the Interior, effective last Thursday night. For me, there are few duties within the Federal Government as important to the American people as executing the varied missions of the Department of the Interior.

Over the course of my career, I have had the chance to serve three different Secretaries of the Interior during nearly a decade of service. I learned a great deal from each of them.

My appreciation and affection for the Department's overarching mission and for all of you who are dedicated to fulfilling that mission is real and deeply felt. To say it was humbling to meet with the President to discuss the Department's mission, and to then be entrusted with leading it, is a significant understatement. Being confirmed by the Senate with bipartisan support is a vote of confidence and trust that carries with it a tremendous obligation to ensure that each decision is well grounded in the law and the facts.

Like many of you, I have an authentic attachment to the many special places managed by the Department for the benefit of our own and future generations. I know and love the rich histories and varied cultures of the Department's Bureaus. I am passionate about the work we do together. I will strive to make our work environment better by listening to and acting upon your suggestions for improvement.

I believe that each person who chooses to work at the Department finds fulfillment in serving the American people. We must also share a common commitment to making the Department not only better, but more effective. We can maintain those values even at those times when we might find our opinions differ—because we are bound together by a common purpose.

Each of the three Secretaries I served brought a unique perspective and approach to their job. I thought it would be helpful to share a few personal perspectives with you as I begin to serve in this new capacity. It is my hope that doing so will give you a better sense of both my perspective and my priorities. I also hope it will help place my future actions in context as I begin to move the Department forward.

Background and Perspective

I grew up in rural western Colorado and spent my summers on my grandparents' ranch in windswept southeastern Wyoming, which fostered my passion for hunting and fishing.

I was raised in an area just east of the small town of Rifle. In that part of Garfield County, the four small communities of Rifle, Silt, New Castle, and Glenwood Springs are located west to east along a valley through which the Colorado River, the railroad, and now Interstate I-70 run. I spent part of my youth in schools in each of these communities. Each are rural towns, essentially surrounded by a significant presence of lands managed by the Forest Service in the White River National Forest and by the Bureau of Land Management. The culture, history, and economy of each of these communities depended on, and still depend on, both the development and the utilization of natural resources, as well as the conservation and recreation associated with those same natural resources.

This area features world-class hunting, gold-medal trout fishing, robust energy development, incredible wilderness areas, great skiing, off-highway vehicle trails, and mountain biking, all within a few miles of each other. Growing up in this environment instilled in me a love and appreciation for the splendor of the outdoors and the magnificence of the natural environment.

In many ways, the history of these communities epitomizes the changes that have occurred in many of the communities that are surrounded by public lands across our country. For example, Glenwood Springs was one of the first communities in the western United States to become a resort town at the dawn of the 20th century. It remains a popular tourist area today, where skiing, rafting, hiking, kayaking, hunting, mountain biking, and every other form of outdoor recreation you can think of are important to the local economy.

The town of New Castle was originally a coal town until 86 miners lost their lives in two explosions caused by methane gas in the late 1800s and early 1900s. Those tragedies ended coal mining in New Castle, but the resulting coal fire has continued to smolder more than 100 years later. It was, and is, a poignant reminder of what a world without common sense environmental or safety regulation would look like.

During my youth, many New Castle residents worked "up-valley" in Glenwood Springs or Aspen. One of my most salient and enduring memories occurred on April 15, 1981, when a close friend's father perished in a mine explosion up-valley that killed 15 miners at the Dutch Creek Mine No. 1. As a result of that tragedy, I witnessed firsthand how much my friend and his brothers missed having a father, and I think of him every time I evaluate a matter related to worker safety at the Department.

The town of Silt was known for its agriculture production. Rifle was known for its ranching, energy booms and busts, and hunting. Energy tax revenues have been important to Rifle, making vital public services available to the community, including an exceptional hospital facility.

Not every day was grand growing up in western Colorado. A large energy company decided to leave the Western Slope after determining that it did not want to proceed forward with a development project. That decision dramatically impacted my community. I recall that about 2,300 people lost their jobs. The day the layoffs were announced became known as Black Sunday.

Watching people struggle—seeing their hopes and dreams falter—crystallized an empathy in me for similarly vulnerable communities. Ultimately, the economic environment was so bad in my community that I decided to get a GED and go to college early so I could strive for a better future. This experience also fostered in me an appreciation of the need for a balanced approach to complex issues involving natural resources. Pursuit of that balance drew me to a career as a natural resource lawyer. It also instilled an understanding that those of us who are entrusted to make decisions on behalf of the public interest must appreciate the actual consequences of our actions before proceeding.

I share these thoughts and experiences with you to highlight my view that our missions are varied for important reasons. Experience has shown me that our decisions have real consequences at both the large-scale and the individual levels.

In most instances, I believe that finding the right balance for these varied missions is best done with significant engagement between our field offices and State and local elected representatives, and with input from local communities. Those of you who work in the field are often the most attuned to local views and have a keen understanding of the consequences actions will have on your neighbors.

This is one reason why I believe we must place more resources, decision-making authority, and accountability closer to the "front lines" of the organization. In taking this approach, we are more likely to arrive at durable, lasting solutions and outcomes that are balanced and minimize the potential for future conflict.

Priorities

For decision makers within the Department, please understand that I expect you to have a thorough knowledge and understanding of the factual and legal setting as well as our actual decision space when making a decision. Our conclusions must be grounded in the facts and the laws as they exist, rather than the facts or laws we might wish to exist to fit a desired policy option.

We can and should expect to have healthy disagreement internally at times. I have always believed that reaching a sound decision on a complex issue often includes listening to and understanding contrary views. I have never been troubled by changing my mind after listening to a new argument that better informed my view. However, it is ultimately the policymaker's job, to the extent he or she has discretion, to exercise that discretion to achieve the Administration's goals, consistent with the facts and the law.

Since returning to the Department in 2017, my focus has been on improvement and execution. My focus has included beginning to fundamentally transform the Departmental and Bureau-level ethics programs to ingrain a culture of ethical compliance and reduce workplace misconduct; moving forward based on the direction and priorities articulated by the President; improving our business processes; and carefully considering suggestions for improvement received from within the organization.

I greatly appreciated the suggestions I have received from you. Going forward, I hope you will continue to share your thoughts of how we can continue to make the Department better. Please share them through the electronic suggestion box at ideas@ios.doi.gov and know that I welcome and consider them.

Over the past 2 years, we have worked hard to implement the President's agenda for the Department. The President has been clear in his direction and priorities. His vision has been expressed through a series of Executive orders and Presidential memoranda detailing goals for the Department, including:

- EO 13781 Comprehensive Plan for Reorganizing the Executive Branch;
- EO 13783 Promoting Energy Independence and Economic Growth;
- EO 13792 Review of Designations Under the Antiquities Act;
- EO 13795 Implementing an America-First Offshore Energy Strategy;
- EO 13807 Establishing Discipline and Accountability in the Environmental Review and Permitting Process for Infrastructure Projects;
- EO 13817 A Federal Strategy to Ensure Secure and Reliable Supplies of Critical Minerals;
- EO 13840 Ocean Policy to Advance the Economic, Security, and Environmental Interests of the United States;
- EO 13855 Promoting Active Management of America's Forests, Rangelands, and other Federal Lands to Improve Conditions and Reduce Wildfire Risk; and
- The Presidential Memorandum on Promoting the Reliable Supply and Delivery of Water in the West.

These orders and memoranda have given the Department very detailed and specific instruction on several issues, and thus have formed the foundation of the Department's objectives since January 2017. As Secretary, one of the duties I am tasked with is moving the Department and its Bureaus forward in a way that effectuates the President's vision, consistent with our legal responsibilities. We have moved forward promptly to implement the President's priorities, and we will continue to do so. This means the Department's leadership team and I will be focused on:

- Enhancing the visitor experience at our National Parks and public lands by better meeting our infrastructure and maintenance needs;
- Delegating greater authority and accountability closer to the front line in our organization and modernizing the Department to better meet the needs of today and tomorrow;
- Working to ensure meaningful consultation and self-determination for Tribes, Alaska Native communities, and our territories;
- Building a meaningful conservation stewardship legacy by expanding public access for sport and recreation opportunities on public lands;
- Collaborating with states to protect and improve the North American Wildlife Conservation Model, while continuing the move toward shared conservation stewardship;
- Modifying or eliminating unneeded and unnecessary regulations;
- Administering the appropriate development of all forms of energy on our Federal lands and the Outer Continental Shelf;
- Ensuring that actions taken by the Department and its Bureaus reflect the development and promotion of a culture of ethical compliance and a workplace free of harassment;
- Implementing the John D. Dingell, Jr. Conservation, Management, and Recreation Act; and
- Modifying our business practices and processes to eliminate unnecessary steps and duplicative reviews, while maintaining rigorous environmental standards.

Reasonable People Can Have Differing Perspectives

As I went through the confirmation process, I saw firsthand how people of different philosophies can find ways to work together to make progress on important issues. I have always believed that people can disagree on important issues without being disagreeable.

As Secretary, I will strive to engage in and maintain communication with both the majority and the minority parties' committee leadership in the House and the Senate in a manner that respects their role in our constitutional form of government. I expect the same from them. I will strive to listen to and understand the views of public officials without challenging their motivations or intentions merely because of a difference in opinion.

I will also strive to address colleagues and citizens in a manner that I hope others would treat our daughters, sons, or partners. I ask you to do the same thing. When we interact with others, particularly the public, we represent the entire Federal Government. What may seem like an unimportant interaction to us in any given moment might be extraordinarily significant to the person with whom we are interacting. The decisions we make can have great consequences for them, and being respectful and decent in our interactions benefits everyone.

Finally, I will continue to regularly communicate with all of you through messages like this one as well as in-person meetings to keep you informed of the Department's priorities and progress. Again, I hope that you will continue to email your own suggestions through the electronic suggestion box.

Conclusion

I hope this message is helpful to you. I look forward to working with each of you as we carry out and balance the multitude of mandates and authorities that make up the organization we call the Department of the Interior. I believe we can and must do so in a way that is good for the natural environment as well as the communities, families, and individuals whose livelihoods depend on our decisions. It is a humbling honor to serve the public in this capacity and to work with you.

Sincerely,
Secretary David L. Bernhardt

ACKNOWLEDGMENTS

The circumstances that led me to present my views on the administrative state came about by accident. I received a call from an acquaintance who was affiliated with the newly established America First Policy Institute (AFPI). He asked if I might be interested in helping him with issues related to regulatory policy. The invitation appealed to me because I believe that our nation's leaders and governmental institutions should be delivering much better outcomes for the American people.

Soon I was telling Brooke Rollins and Linda McMahon that I would like to assist them in some way at AFPI. This in turn brought me to reconnect with James Sherk, the executive director of AFPI's Center for American Freedom, where I now serve as chairman. Together we developed a vision for the Center, formulated a policy focus, and implemented an agenda. James also collaborated with me to make this book possible. He is an extraordinary young man with a bright future, and I have enjoyed working with him.

A mutual friend of ours connected me with Caitlin Styrsky, who is the deputy policy editor at Ballotpedia. This effort would not have come to fruition without her many hours of talking through ideas, researching facts, and reviewing drafts. Her assistance is deeply appreciated.

In addition, I owe a great debt to my wife, Gena, who has put up with my forays into public service and was willing to read and provide helpful comments on multiple drafts when there were many other things she would have preferred doing.

The folks at Encounter Books, particularly Carol Staswick, added clarity and greatly improved the manuscript. I am grateful for their willingness to take on the project.

This book reflects the lessons I have learned from having the great privilege of serving the American people under two presidents, alongside dozens of other political appointees who served at the Department of the Interior in either the George W. Bush or the Donald J. Trump administration. I am thankful for the opportunity to work together with them. Likewise, I greatly appreciate the dedicated career public servants at the Department of the Interior who took care to check their political leanings at the door and honorably fulfilled their duty to serve the American people.

NOTES

CHAPTER 1—GROWTH OF THE FEDERAL GOVERNMENT

1 Lisa Rein, "Civil War gave birth to much of modern federal government," *Washington Post*, October 7, 2011, https://www.washingtonpost.com/politics/civil-war-gave-birth-to-much-of-modern-federal-government/2011/09/22/gIQA43EFSL_story.html.

2 National Park Service, "Industry and Economy during the Civil War," last modified August 23, 2017, https://www.nps.gov/articles/industry-and-economy-during-the-civil-war.htm.

3 An Act to establish a Department of Agriculture, May 15, 1862, 37th Cong. (1861–1862), *Public Acts of the 37th Congress*, chap. 72, *United States Statutes at Large*, vol. 12, 387, https://memory.loc.gov/cgi-bin/ampage?collId=llsl&fileName=012/llsl012.db&recNum=418.

4 Woodrow Wilson, *The State: Elements of Historical and Practical Politics* (Boston: D.C. Heath & Co., 1889), 305.

5 Woodrow Wilson, *Constitutional Government in the United States* (New York: Columbia University Press, 1908), 57.

6 Woodrow Wilson, "The Study of Administration," *Political Science Quarterly* 2, no. 2 (June 1887): 217.

7 Ibid., 216.

8 Edward Glaeser and Andrei Schleifer, "The Rise of the Regulatory State," *Journal of Economic Literature* 41, no. 2 (2003): 401–25, https://dash.harvard.edu/bitstream/handle/1/30747197/w8650.pdf?sequence=1.

9 James Madison, *Federalist* no. 47 (February 1, 1788), https://avalon.law.yale.edu/18th_century/fed47.asp.

CHAPTER 2—UNACCOUNTABLE BUREAUCRACY

1 The Canadian Press, "Downtrodden in D.C.: Federal employees are in tears with the reality of working for Donald Trump," *National Post*, December 10, 2016, https://nationalpost.com/news/world/downtrodden-in-d-c-federal-employees-are-in-tears-with-the-reality-of-working-for-donald-trump.

2 Christopher Flavelle and Benjamin Bain, "Washington Bureaucrats Are Quietly Working to Undermine Trump's Agenda," Bloomberg, December 18, 2017, https://www.bloomberg.com/news/features/2017-12-18/washington-bureaucrats-are-chipping-away-at-trump-s-agenda.

3   Juliet Eilperin, Lisa Rein, and Marc Fisher, "Resistance from within: Federal workers push back against Trump," *Washington Post*, January 31, 2017, https://www.washingtonpost.com/politics/resistance-from-within-federal-workers-push-back-against-trump/2017/01/31/c65b110e-e7cb-11e6-b82f-687d6e6a3e7c_story.html.

4   U.S. Department of the Interior, Office of Inspector General, "Review of U.S. Park Police Actions at Lafayette Park," June 8, 2021, https://web.archive.org/web/20210609181941/https://www.doioig.gov/reports/review-us-park-police-actions-lafayette-park.

5   Daniel Feller, "Andrew Jackson: Domestic Affairs," Miller Center, University of Virginia, accessed April 2022, https://millercenter.org/president/jackson/domestic-affairs.

6   Gerald E. Frug, "Does the Constitution Prevent the Discharge of Civil Service Employees?" *University of Pennsylvania Law Review* 124, no. 4 (1976): 955, https://scholarship.law.upenn.edu/cgi/viewcontent.cgi?article=4997&context=penn_law_review.

7   Equal Employment Opportunity Commission, Table B-10, FY 2019, Total Number and Average Processing Days for All Complaint Closures, https://www.eeoc.gov/sites/default/files/2021-07/2019%20Annual%20Report%20Complaints%20Tables.zip.

8   U.S. Merit Systems Protection Board, Office of Policy and Evaluation, "Removing Poor Performers in the Federal Service," Issue Paper, September 1995, 2, https://www.mspb.gov/studies/studies/Removing_Poor_Performers_in_the_Federal_Service_Issue_Paper_September_1995_253662.pdf.

9   U.S. Office of Personnel Management, Office of Merit Systems Oversight and Effectiveness, *Poor Performers in Government: A Quest for the True Story*, Report of a Special Study, January 1999, 11, https://archive.opm.gov/studies/perform.pdf.

10 U.S. Merit Systems Protection Board, Office of Policy and Evaluation, "Remedying Unacceptable Employee Performance in the Federal Civil Service," Research Brief, June 18, 2019, https://www.mspb.gov/studies/researchbriefs/Remedying_Unacceptable_Employee_Performance_in_the_Federal_Civil_Service_1627610.pdf.

11 James Sherk, "Increasing Accountability in the Civil Service," Center for American Freedom, May 26, 2021, https://americafirstpolicy.com/assets/uploads/files/civilservicereform.pdf.

12 Jorg L. Spenkuch, Edoardo Teso, and Guo Xu, "Ideology and Performance in Public Organizations," National Bureau of Economic Research, Working Paper 28673, April 2021, https://www.nber.org/system/files/working_papers/w28673/w28673.pdf.

13 Brian D. Feinstein and Abby K. Wood, "Divided Agencies," *Southern California Law Review*, forthcoming (last revised April 21, 2022), https://papers.ssrn.com/sol3/papers.cfm?abstract_id=3925861.

14 James Sherk, "Tales from the Swamp," America First Policy, February 1, 2021,

https://americafirstpolicy.com/assets/uploads/files/Tales_from_the_swamp.pdf.

15 Deborah Birx, *Silent Invasion: The Untold Story of the Trump Administration, Covid-19, and Preventing the Next Pandemic Before It's Too Late* (New York: Harper, 2022).

16 Monmouth University Polling Institute, "Public Troubled by Deep State," March 19, 2018, https://www.monmouth.edu/polling-institute/reports/monmouthpoll_us_031918/.

17 Lisa Rein, "Civil War gave birth to much of modern federal government," *Washington Post*, October 7, 2011, https://www.washingtonpost.com/politics/civil-war-gave-birth-to-much-of-modern-federal-government/2011/09/22/gIQA43EFSL_story.html.

CHAPTER 3—UNELECTED RULE MAKERS

1 "Endangered and Threatened Wildlife and Plants; Designation of Revised Critical Habitat for the Northern Spotted Owl," 77 Fed. Reg. 71875, 71877 (December 4, 2012), https://www.federalregister.gov/documents/2012/12/04/2012-28714/endangered-and-threatened-wildlife-and-plants-designation-of-revised-critical-habitat-for-the.

2 "Interagency Cooperation–Endangered Species Act of 1973," 43 Fed. Reg. 869, 872 (January 4, 1978).

3 Tennessee Valley Authority v. Hill, 437 U.S. 153 (1978).

4 House Merchant Marine and Fisheries Committee, H.R. Rep. No. 95-1625, at 17.

5 "Endangered and Threatened Wildlife and Plants; Revised Designation of Critical Habitat for the Northern Spotted Owl," 85 Fed. Reg. 48487 (August 11, 2020), https://www.federalregister.gov/documents/2020/08/11/2020-15675/endangered-and-threatened-wildlife-and-plants-revised-designation-of-critical-habitat-for-the.

6 16 U.S.C. §§ 1532(13), 1538(a)(1)(B), 1540(a), (b).

7 16 U.S.C. § 1532(19) (definition of "take"); 50 CFR § 222.102 (definition of "harm").

8 "Endangered and Threatened Wildlife and Plants; 12-Month Finding for the Northern Spotted Owl," 85 Fed. Reg. 81145 (December 15, 2020), https://www.federalregister.gov/documents/2020/12/15/2020-27198/endangered-and-threatened-wildlife-and-plants-12-month-finding-for-the-northern-spotted-owl.

9 "Endangered and Threatened Wildlife and Plants; Revised Designation of Critical Habitat for the Northern Spotted Owl," 86 Fed. Reg. 4820 (January 15, 2021), https://www.federalregister.gov/documents/2021/01/15/2021-00484/endangered-and-threatened-wildlife-and-plants-revised-designation-of-critical-habitat-for-the.

10 Ballotpedia, *The Administrative State: A Primer*, chap. 1, https://ballotpedia.s3.amazonaws.com/images/d/d6/TASP_Primer_Final.pdf.

11 National Federation of Independent Business v. OSHA, Nos. 21A244 and 21A247, 595 U.S. ___ (2022), https://www.law.cornell.edu/supremecourt/text/21A244.

12 Wayman v. Southard, 23 U.S. 1 (1825), https://supreme.justia.com/cases/federal/us/23/1/.

13 Ballotpedia, *The Administrative State: A Primer*, 24–25.

14 J. W. Hampton, Jr. & Co. v. United States, 276 U.S. 394 (1928), https://supreme.justia.com/cases/federal/us/276/394/.

15 Panama Refining Co. v. Ryan, 293 U.S. 388 (1935), https://supreme.justia.com/cases/federal/us/293/388/; and A. L. A. Schechter Poultry Corp. v. United States, 295 U.S. 495 (1935), https://supreme.justia.com/cases/federal/us/295/495.

16 *Schechter*, 295 U.S.

17 Ballotpedia, *The Administrative State: A Primer*, 26.

18 Gundy v. United States, No. 17-6086, 588 U.S. ___ (2019), https://caselaw.findlaw.com/us-supreme-court/17-6086.html.

19 *National Federation of Business v. OSHA.*

20 Teaching American History, "Report on the President's Committee on Administrative Management (The Brownlow Committee Report)," https://teachingamericanhistory.org/document/report-of-the-presidents-committee-on-administrative-management-the-brownlow-committee-report/.

21 United States v. Florida East Coast Railway, 410 U.S. 224 (1973), https://supreme.justia.com/cases/federal/us/410/224/.

22 Perez v. Mortgage Bankers Association, 575 U.S. 92 (2015), https://www.law.cornell.edu/supremecourt/text/13-1041.

23 Joseph Postell, "'The People Surrender Nothing': Social Compact Theory, Republicanism, and the Modern Administrative State," *Missouri Law Review* 81, no. 4 (2016), https://scholarship.law.missouri.edu/mlr/vol81/iss4/8/.

24 James Sherk, "Tales from the Swamp," America First Policy, February 1, 2021, https://americafirstpolicy.com/assets/uploads/files/Tales_from_the_swamp.pdf.

25 Save Our Sonoran, Inc., v. Flowers, 408 F.3d 1113 (9th Cir. 2004), https://caselaw.findlaw.com/us-9th-circuit/1371564.html.

26 43 U.S.C., Public Lands, https://www.law.cornell.edu/uscode/text/43.

27 50 CFR 402, Interagency Cooperation–Endangered Species Act of 1973, As Amended, https://www.govinfo.gov/app/details/CFR-2012-title50-vol11/CFR-2012-title50-vol11-part402.

28 50 CFR 402.02.

29 50 CFR 402.14.

30 National Academy of Science, *Assessing Risks to Endangered and Threatened Species from Pesticides* (Washington, D.C.: The National Academies Press, 2015), 95, https://nap.nationalacademies.org/download/18344.

31 U.S. Department of the Interior, Office of Inspector General, "Investigative

Report of Alleged Improper Influence by the Secretary of the Interior in the FWS's Scientific Process," Report No. 19-0434, December 10, 2019.

32 U.S. Fish and Wildlife Service, "Frequently Asked Questions: U.S. Fish and Wildlife Service Proposal to List Polar Bears as Threatened Species," June 2001, USFWS National Digital Library, https://digitalmedia.fws.gov/digital/collection/document/id/91/.

33 "Endangered and Threatened Wildlife and Plants; Determination of Threatened Status for the Polar Bear (*Ursus maritimus*) Throughout Its Range," 73 Fed. Reg. 28211 (May 15, 2008), https://www.federalregister.gov/documents/2008/05/15/E8-11105/endangered-and-threatened-wildlife-and-plants-determination-of-threatened-status-for-the-polar-bear.

34 Administrative Conference of the United States, "Recommendation 92-2: Agency Policy Statements," June 18, 1992, https://www.acus.gov/sites/default/files/documents/92-2.pdf.

35 William Funk, "The Dilemma of Nonlegislative Rules," Administrative Law Jotwell, June 3, 2011, https://adlaw.jotwell.com/the-dilemma-of-nonlegislative-rules/.

36 Exec. Order 13891, October 9, 2019, "Promoting the Rule of Law Through Improved Agency Guidance Documents," 84 Fed. Reg. 55235 (October 15, 2019), https://www.federalregister.gov/documents/2019/10/15/2019-22623/promoting-the-rule-of-law-through-improved-agency-guidance-documents.

37 Bureau of Land Management, "Climate Change Listening Sessions: A Structured Brainstorming Activity with BLM Employees," March 2022, https://subscriber.politicopro.com/eenews/f/eenews/?id=0000017f-9e4a-d07e-af7f-9e6aaa470000.

38 West Virginia v. Environmental Protection Agency, No. 20-1530, 597 U.S. ___ (2022), https://www.law.cornell.edu/supremecourt/text/20-1530.

39 Ibid.

CHAPTER 4—THE ENFORCERS

1 Ballotpedia, "Administrative law judge," accessed September 19, 2022, https://ballotpedia.org/Administrative_law_judge.

2 Herring v. New York, 422 U.S. 853, 862 (1975) ("[T]he very premise of our adversary system of criminal justice is that partisan advocacy on both sides of a case will best promote the ultimate objective that the guilty be convicted and the innocent go free.").

3 5 U.S.C. §§ 551 *et seq.*

4 Ballotpedia, "Administrative law judge."

5 Gretchen Morgenson, "At the S.E.C., a Question of Home-Court Edge," *New York Times*, October 5, 2013, https://www.nytimes.com/2013/10/06/business/at-the-sec-a-question-of-home-court-edge.html.

6 Jean Eaglesham, "SEC Wins With In-House Judges," *Wall Street Journal*, May 6, 2015, https://www.wsj.com/articles/sec-wins-with-in-house-judges-1430965803.

7   Lucia v. Securities and Exchange Commission, No. 17-130, 585 U.S. ___ (2018), https://www.supremecourt.gov/opinions/17pdf/17-130_4f14.pdf.

8   Exec. Order 13843, July 10, 2018, "Excepting Administrative Law Judges from the Competitive Service," 83 Fed. Reg. 32755 (July 13, 2018), https://www.federalregister.gov/documents/2018/07/13/2018-15202/excepting-administrative-law-judges-from-the-competitive-servicent-federal-operations.

9   The appointments clause allows Congress to vest the authority to appoint "Officers of the United States" in agency heads instead of the president. It does not give Congress authority to subdelegate these appointments to agency staff. Competitive service ALJ hiring procedures required agencies to pick from the top three ALJ candidates, as determined by OPM staff. This severely constrained the discretion of agency heads and gave OPM career staff a larger role in ALJ selection than agency heads. Once the Supreme Court determined that ALJs were constitutional officers, it was not clear that these constraints on agency head discretion were consistent with the appointments clause.

10 Free Enterprise Fund v. Public Company Accounting Oversight Board, 561 U.S. 477 (2010).

11 Jarkesy v. Securities and Exchange Commission, 34 F.4th 446 (5th Cir. 2022), https://www.ca5.uscourts.gov/opinions/pub/20/20-61007-CV0.pdf.

12 Kent Barnett, "Why Bias Challenges to Administrative Adjudication Should Succeed," *Missouri Law Review* 81 (2016), https://scholarship.law.missouri.edu/mlr/vol81/iss4/9/.

13 Michael Asimow, ed., *A Guide to Federal Agency Adjudication*, Section of Administrative Law and Regulatory Practice, American Bar Association (Chicago: ABA Publishing, 2003), https://books.google.com/books?id=LGgxW5yi4rQC&printsec=frontcover&source=gbs_ge_summary_r&cad=0#v=onepage&q&f=false.

14 Jennifer L. Selin and David E. Lewis, *Sourcebook of United States Executive Agencies*, 2nd ed., October 2018, Administrative Conference of the United States, https://www.acus.gov/sites/default/files/documents/ACUS%20Sourcebook%20of%20Executive%20Agenices%202d%20ed.%20508%20Compliant.pdf.

15 Securities and Exchange Commission v. Chenery Corp., 332 U.S. 194 (1947), https://www.law.cornell.edu/supremecourt/text/332/194.

16 Ibid.

17 William Mayton, "The Legislative Resolution of the Rulemaking Versus Adjudication Problem in Agency Lawmaking," *Duke Law Journal* 1980, no. 1 (February): 103–35, http://scholarship.law.duke.edu/cgi/viewcontent.cgi?article=2732&context=dlj.

18 Barnett, "Why Bias Challenges to Administrative Adjudication Should Succeed."

19 "Federal Objections Overcome, Beach Fill Projects Can Proceed in 3 Municipalities," *Cape May County Herald*, November 4, 2019, https://www.

capemaycountyherald.com/news/environment/federal-objections-overcome-beachfill-projects-can-proceed-in-3-municipalities/article_47836054-ff59-11e9-ad45-c31717434b2f.html.

20 Paul R. Verkuil, "Reflections upon the Federal Administrative Judiciary," College of William & Mary Law School Scholarship Repository, 1992, http://scholarship.law.wm.edu/cgi/viewcontent.cgi?article=2062&context=facpubs.

21 Philip Hamburger, *Is Administrative Law Unlawful?* (Chicago: University of Chicago Press, 2015).

22 Anonymous v. Baker, 360 U.S. 287 (1959), https://caselaw.findlaw.com/us-supreme-court/360/287.html.

23 Denezpi v. United States, 596 U. S. ____ (2022), https://www.supremecourt.gov/opinions/21pdf/20-7622_ljgm.pdf.

24 Ibid., Gorsuch dissenting, 13.

25 Ibid.

26 Ibid., 1.

27 Ibid., 11, citing 58 Fed. Reg. 54407 (1993).

28 Ibid.

29 25 CFR §§ 11.400–11.454 (2021).

30 25 CFR § 11.449.

31 U.S. Department of the Interior, Bureau of Indian Affairs, Court of Indian Offenses Serving the Kewa Pueblo (Previously Listed as the Pueblo of Santo Domingo), 85 Fed. Reg. 10714 (February 25, 2020).

32 25 CFR § 11.202.1

33 25 CFR § 11.204.

34 *Denezpi*, Gorsuch dissenting, 13, citing Murray's Lessee v. Hoboken Land & Improvement Co., 18 How. 272, 277 (1856).

35 *Jarkesy*, 34 F.4th 446.

36 Todd Gaziano, Jonathan Wood, and Elizabeth Slattery, "The Regulatory State's Due Process Deficits," Pacific Legal Foundation, May 2020, https://pacificlegal.org/wp-content/uploads/2020/05/The-Regulatory-State-Due-Process-Deficits-May-2020.pdf.

37 Pacific Legal Foundation, "PLF forces EPA to stop harassing farmer over environmentally friendly stock pond," accessed November 22, 2022, https://pacificlegal.org/case/johnson-v-environmental-protection-agency/.

38 Sackett v. Envt'l Protection Agency, 566 U.S. 120 (2012).

39 Sackett v. Envt'l Protection Agency, 8 F.4th 1075 (9th Cir. 2021), cert granted January 24, 2022.

40 Exec. Order 13924, May 19, 2020, "Regulatory Relief to Support Economic Recovery," 85 Fed. Reg. 31353 (May 22, 2020), https://www.federalregister.gov/documents/2020/05/22/2020-11301/regulatory-relief-to-support-economic-recovery.

CHAPTER 5—ABSENT JUDGES AND A WEAK CONGRESS

1 State of Wyoming v. U.S. Department of the Interior, 2016 WL 3509415 (D. Wyo. June 21, 2016), https://nill.narf.org/bulletins/federal/documents/wyoming_v_interior_june2016.html.

2 State of California v. Bureau of Land Management, No. 18-CV-00521-HSG, 2020 WL 1492708 (N.D. Cal. Mar. 27, 2020), https://narf.org/nill/bulletins/federal/documents/cal_v_blm_v_zinke.html.

3 21 CFR § 10.45, https://www.law.cornell.edu/cfr/text/21/10.45.

4 American School of Magnetic Healing v. McAnnulty, 187 U.S. 94 (1902), https://supreme.justia.com/cases/federal/us/187/94/.

5 Edward D. Re, "Due Process, Judicial Review, and the Rights of the Individual," *Cleveland State Law Review* 39, no. 1 (1991), https://engagedscholarship.csuohio.edu/cgi/viewcontent.cgi?article=1779&context=clevstlrev.

6 Abbott Laboratories v. Gardner, 387 U.S. 136 (1967).

7 Guedes v. Bureau of Alcohol, Tobacco, Firearms, and Explosives, No. 21-5045 (D.C. Cir. Aug. 9, 2022), https://casetext.com/case/guedes-v-bureau-of-alcohol-tobacco-firearms-explosives-1.

8 James Landis, *The Administrative Process* (New Haven: Yale University Press, 1938), https://books.google.com/books/about/The_Administrative_Process.html?id=FXRDAAAAIAAJ.

9 Antonin Scalia, "Judicial Deference to Administrative Interpretations of Law," *Duke Law Journal* 1989, no. 3 (June): 511–21, https://scholarship.law.duke.edu/cgi/viewcontent.cgi?article=3075&context=dlj.

10 Chevron USA Inc. v. Natural Resources Defense Council, 467 U.S. 837 (1984), https://supreme.justia.com/cases/federal/us/467/837.

11 Scalia, "Judicial Deference to Administrative Interpretations of Law."

12 Skidmore v. Swift & Co., 323 U.S. 134 (1944), https://supreme.justia.com/cases/federal/us/323/134/.

13 Christensen v. Harris County, 529 U.S. 576 (2000), https://supreme.justia.com/cases/federal/us/529/576/.

14 Bowles v. Seminole Rock & Sand Co., 325 U.S. 410 (1945), https://supreme.justia.com/cases/federal/us/325/410/.

15 Kisor v. Wilkie, No. 18-15, 588 U.S. ___ (2019), https://supreme.justia.com/cases/federal/us/588/18-15/.

16 Scalia, "Judicial Deference to Administrative Interpretations of Law."

17 Cynthia R. Farina, "Statutory Interpretation and the Balance of Power in the Administrative State," *Columbia Law Review* 89, no. 3 (April 1989): 452–528, https://scholarship.law.cornell.edu/cgi/viewcontent.cgi?article=1560&context=facpub.

18 Christopher J. Walker, "Attacking Auer and Chevron Deference: A Literature Review," *Georgetown Journal of Law & Public Policy* 16 (2018): 103–22, https://www.law.georgetown.edu/public-policy-journal/wp-content/uploads/sites/23/2018/05/16-1-Attacking-Auer-and-Chevron-Deference.pdf.

19 Steven Davidoff Solomon, "Should Agencies Decide Law? Doctrine May Be Tested at Gorsuch Hearing," *New York Times*, March 14, 2017, https://www.nytimes.com/2017/03/14/business/dealbook/neil-gorsuch-chevron-deference.html.

20 Michael Kagan, "Loud and Soft Anti-Chevron Decisions," UNLV William S. Boyd School of Law, *Scholarly Works*, 2018, 1142, https://scholars.law.unlv.edu/facpub/1142/.

21 Michigan v. Environmental Protection Agency, 576 U.S. 743 (2015), https://supreme.justia.com/cases/federal/us/576/14-46/.

22 *Kisor*, 588 U.S.

23 Ibid.

24 Kagan, "Loud and Soft Anti-Chevron Decisions."

25 David B. Rivkin Jr. and Mark Wendell DeLaquil, "No More Deference to the Administrative State," *Wall Street Journal*, July 10, 2022, https://www.wsj.com/articles/no-more-deference-to-the-administrative-state-west-virginia-v-epa-chevron-major-questions-john-roberts-regulation-democracy-congress-11657475255.

26 Justin R. Pidor and Courtney McVean, "Environmental Settlements and Administrative Law," *Harvard Environmental Law Review* 39 (2015): 191–239, https://papers.ssrn.com/sol3/papers.cfm?abstract_id=2425990.

27 Jamie Conrad, "We Shouldn't Dismiss 'Sue and Settle' - or Other Regulatory Problems," *Regulatory Review*, May 18, 2015, https://www.theregreview.org/2015/05/18/conrad-sue-and-settle/.

28 Andrew Grossman, "Regulation Through Sham Litigation: The Sue and Settle Phenomenon," The Heritage Foundation, February 25, 2014, http://www.heritage.org/crime-and-justice/report/regulation-through-sham-litigation-the-sue-and-settle-phenomenon.

29 The Secretary of the Interior, Order No. 3688, "Promoting Transparency and Accountability in Consent Decrees and Settlement Agreements," U.S. Department of the Interior, September 11, 2018, https://www.doi.gov/sites/doi.gov/files/elips/documents/so_3368_promoting_transparency_and_accountability_in_consent_decrees_and_settlement_agreements_0.pdf.

30 U.S. Chamber of Commerce, *Sue and Settle Update: Damage Done, 2013–2016*, May 2017, https://www.uschamber.com/assets/archived/images/u.s._chamber_sue_and_settle_2017_updated_report.pdf.

31 U.S. Chamber of Commerce, *Sue and Settle: Regulating Behind Closed Doors*, May 2013, https://www.uschamber.com/sites/default/files/documents/files/SUEANDSETTLEREPORT-Final.pdf.

32 Environmental Protection Agency, "Administrator Pruitt Issues Directive to End EPA 'Sue & Settle,'" October 16, 2017, https://www.epa.gov/newsreleases/administrator-pruitt-issues-directive-end-epa-sue-settle.

33 Clark Mindock, "Interior to reconsider social cost of greenhouse gas in Dakota oil leases," Reuters, September 7, 2022, https://www.reuters.com/legal/government/interior-reconsider-social-cost-greenhouse-gas-dakota-oil-leases-2022-09-07/.

CHAPTER 6—THE CHIEF EXECUTIVE

1   Don Devine, *Political Management of the Bureaucracy*, 2nd ed. (Ottawa, Ill.: Jameson Books, Inc., 2017), 116.

2   Robert Reich, *Locked in the Cabinet* (New York: Knopf, 1997), 110.

3   Alexander Hamilton, *Federalist* no. 70 (March 18, 1788), https://avalon.law. yale.edu/18th_century/fed70.asp.

4   Ibid.

5   Edmond v. United States, 20 U.S. 651 (1997), https://supreme.justia.com/ cases/federal/us/520/651/.

6   United States v. Arthrex, Inc., No. 19-1434, 594 U.S. ___ (2021), https:// supreme.justia.com/cases/federal/us/594/19-1434/.

7   Myers v. United States, 272 U.S. 52 (1926), https://supreme.justia.com/cases/ federal/us/272/52/.

8   Humphrey's Executor v. United States, 295 U.S. 602 (1935), https://supreme. justia.com/cases/federal/us/295/602/.

9   Leu v. International Boundary Commission, 605 F.3d 693 (9th Cir. 2010), https://caselaw.findlaw.com/us-9th-circuit/1524533.html.

10 Devine, *Political Management of the Bureaucracy*, 7.

11 Elena Kagan, "Presidential Administration," *Harvard Law Review* 114, no. 8 (June 2001)): 2245–385, https://cdn.harvardlawreview.org/wp-content/ uploads/pdfs/vol114_kagan.pdf.

12 Exec. Order 13771, January 30, 2017, "Reducing Regulation and Controlling Regulatory Costs," 82 Fed. Reg. 9339 (February 3, 2017), https://www. federalregister.gov/documents/2017/02/03/2017-02451/reducing-regulation- and-controlling-regulatory-costs.

13 Exec. Order 13777, February 24, 2017, "Enforcing the Regulatory Reform Agenda," 82 Fed. Reg. 12285 (March 1, 2017), https://www.federalregister.gov/ documents/2017/03/01/2017-04107/enforcing-the-regulatory-reform-agenda.

14 Exec. Order 13807, August 15, 2017, "Establishing Discipline and Accountability in the Environmental Review and Permitting Process for Infrastructure Projects," 82 Fed. Reg. 40463 (August 24, 2017), https://www. govinfo.gov/content/pkg/FR-2017-08-24/pdf/2017-18134.pdf.

15 Ibid., 40468.

16 Ibid., 40464.

17 Ibid., 40463.

18 The Secretary of the Interior, Order No. 3355, "Streamlining National Environmental Policy Act Reviews and Implementation of Executive Order 13807, 'Establishing Discipline and Accountability in the Environmental Review and Permitting Process for Infrastructure Projects,'" U.S. Department of the Interior, August 31, 2017.

19 State of Louisiana v. Biden, No. 22-30087 (5th Cir. 2022), https://dockets. justia.com/docket/circuit-courts/ca5/22-30087.

20 State of Louisiana et al. v. Joseph R. Biden et al., No. 2:21-CV-00778, 2022 WL 3570933 (W.D. La. Aug. 18, 2022), https://content.govdelivery.com/

attachments/MTAG/2022/08/19/file_attachments/2248335/Doughty%20
Order%20Oil&Gas.pdf.

21 Exec. Order 12866, September 30, 1993, "Regulatory Planning and Review,"
58 Fed. Reg. 51735 (October 4, 1993), https://www.archives.gov/files/federal-
register/executive-orders/pdf/12866.pdf.

CHAPTER 7—DRAINING THE SWAMP

1 5 U.S.C. § 2301(b)(6), https://www.law.cornell.edu/uscode/text/5/2301.

2 Exec. Order 13839, May 25, 2018, "Promoting Accountability and
Streamlining Removal Procedures Consistent With Merit System
Principles," 83 Fed. Reg. 25343 (June 1, 2018), https://www.federalregister.
gov/documents/2018/06/01/2018-11939/promoting-accountability-and-
streamlining-removal-procedures-consistent-with-merit-system-principles.

3 5 U.S.C. 43, Performance Appraisal, https://www.law.cornell.edu/uscode/
text/5/part-III/subpart-C/chapter-43.

4 U.S. Government Accountability Office, *Federal Workforce: Improved
Supervision and Better Use of Probationary Periods Are Needed to Address
Substandard Employee Performance*, Report to the Chairman, Committee on
Homeland Security and Governmental Affairs, U.S. Senate, February 2015, 25,
https://www.gao.gov/assets/gao-15-191.pdf.

5 U.S. Merit Systems Protection Board, "Why Is the CSRA's Provision for
Removing Poor Performers Not Used More Often?" *Issues of Merit*, August
2018, 4, https://www.mspb.gov/studies/newsletters/Issues_of_Merit_
August_2018_1540524.pdf.

6 5 U.S.C. § 4302(c)(6), https://www.law.cornell.edu/uscode/text/5/4302.

7 "Guidance on PIPs," posted by the Deputy Commandant for Mission
Support, U.S. Coast Guard, https://view.officeapps.live.com/op/view.
aspx?src=https%3A%2F%2Fwww.dcms.uscg.mil%2FPortals%2F10%2FCG-
1%2Fcg121%2Fdocs%2FPerformance%2FPIP_GUIDANCE_WREL.
doc%3Fver%3D2017-03-23-143149-997&wdOrigin=BROWSELINK.

8 See U.S. Merit Systems Protection Board, Woebcke v. DHS, 114 M.S.P.R. 100
(2010); Lewis v. DVA, 113 M.S.P.R. 657 (2010); Villada v. USPS, 115 M.S.P.R.
268 (2010).

9 *Woebcke.*

10 U.S. Merit Systems Protection Board, Boucher v. U.S. Postal Service,
118 M.S.P.R. 640, November 15, 2012, https://www.mspb.gov/decisions/
precedential/BOUCHER_MARIA_THERESA_AT_0752_10_0453_B_1_
OPINION_AND_ORDER_773207.pdf.

11 Agencies do not have to use competitive service hiring procedures to
reinstate former civil service employees. See 5 CFR § 315.401.

12 Agencies could agree to clean-record settlements for nonfederal employers,
but not other federal agencies.

13 Exec. Orders 13836, 13837, and 13839, October 11, 2019, "Memorandum for the
Heads of Executive Departments and Agencies," 82 Fed. Reg. 56095 (October
21, 2019), https://www.federalregister.gov/documents/2019/10/21/2019-23021/
executive-orders-13836-13837-and-13839.

14 5 U.S.C. § 7131(a), https://www.law.cornell.edu/uscode/text/5/7131.

15 U.S. Office of Personnel Management, "OPM Director Implementing President's New Policies to Elevate Federal Government Operations and Protect American Taxpayers," May 25, 2018, https://www.opm.gov/news/releases/2018/05/opm-director-implementing-president-s-new-policies-to-elevate-federal-government-operations-and-protect-american-taxpayers/.

16 "U.S. Department of Veterans Affairs Secretary Clarifies Collective Bargaining Authority Related to Professional Conduct, Patient Care," *Light to Guide Our Feet*, August 17, 2018, https://forum.ltgof.net/node/1582.

17 U.S. Office of Personnel Management, "FY 2016 Official Time Report Highlighting Taxpayer Funded Union Time Released by the U.S. Office of Personnel Management," May 17, 2018, https://www.opm.gov/news/releases/2018/05/fy-2016-official-time-report-highlighting-taxpayer-funded-union-time-released-by-the-us-office-of-personnel-management/.

18 Interior's rate was 0.88 hours in 2016. U.S. Office of Personnel Management, "Official Time Usage in the Federal Government, Fiscal Year 2016," May 2018, https://www.opm.gov/policy-data-oversight/labor-management-relations/reports-on-official-time/reports/2016-official-time-usage-in-the-federal-government.pdf.

19 National Treasury Employees Union, "Executive Orders Attempt to Weaken Civil Service, Disrupt Agency Workplaces," Press Release, May 29, 2018, https://www.nteu.org/media-center/news-releases/2018/05/29/executive-orders.

20 Noam Scheiber, "Trump Moves to Ease the Firing of Federal Workers," *New York Times*, May 25, 2018, https://www.nytimes.com/2018/05/25/business/economy/trump-federal-workers.html.

21 Nicole Ogrysko, "AFGE's top leader resigns amid months-long sexual harassment investigation," Federal News Network, February 28, 2020, https://federalnewsnetwork.com/unions/2020/02/afges-top-leader-resigns-amid-months-long-sexual-harassment-investigation/.

22 Nicole Ogrysko, "Victims sue AFGE over union's handling of former national president's misconduct," Federal News Network, July 7, 2020, https://federalnewsnetwork.com/unions/2020/07/victims-sue-afge-over-unions-handling-of-former-national-presidents-misconduct/.

23 The survey showed that 51 percent of federal workers supported or strongly supported making it easier to remove poorly performing or malfeasant employees. Another 24 percent opposed such efforts, while 24 percent said they were neutral or didn't know about the changes. Erich Wagner, "Survey: Half of Feds Support White House Attempts to Ease Firing Process," *Government Executive*, June 8, 2018, https://www.govexec.com/management/2018/06/survey-half-feds-support-trump-efforts-firing/148818/.

24 U.S. Office of Personnel Management, *Federal Employee Viewpoint Survey*, Governmentwide Management Report, 2020, 11, https://www.opm.gov/fevs/reports/governmentwide-reports/governmentwide-management-report/

governmentwide-report/2020/2020-governmentwide-management-report.
pdf.

25 Ibid., 24.

26 Erich Wagner, "Republican Lawmakers Ask Trump to Repeal Workforce
    Executive Orders," *Government Executive*, June 13, 2018, https://www.govexec.
    com/management/2018/06/republican-lawmakers-ask-trump-repeal-
    workforce-executive-orders/148969/.

27 Erich Wagner, "House Democrats Join Fight Against Workforce Executive
    Orders," *Government Executive*, June 14, 2018, https://www.govexec.com/
    management/2018/06/house-democrats-ask-trump-rescind-workforce-
    executive-orders/149018/.

28 Thunder Basin Coal Co. v. Reich, 510 U.S. 200 (1994), https://supreme.justia.
    com/cases/federal/us/510/200/.

29 Am. Fed'n of Gov't Emps., AFL-CIO v. Trump, 318 F. Supp. 3d 370 (D.D.C.
    2018), https://casetext.com/case/am-fedn-of-govt-emps-v-trump.

30 Am. Fed'n of Gov't Emps., AFL-CIO v. Trump, 929 F.3d 748 (D.C. Cir. 2019),
    https://casetext.com/case/am-fedn-of-govt-emps-v-trump-1.

31 Am. Fed'n of Gov't Emps., AFL-CIO v. Trump, No. 18-5289, U.S. Court of
    Appeals for the D.C. Circuit, September 25, 2019, https://federalnewsnetwork.
    com/wp-content/uploads/2019/09/092519_appeals_rehearing_denied_FNN.
    pdf.

32 Service Employees Intern. Union Local 200 v. Trump, 419 F. Supp. 3d 612
    (W.D.N.Y. 2019), https://casetext.com/case/serv-emps-intl-union-local-200-
    united-v-trump.

33 Ibid.

34 National Association of Agriculture Employees v. Trump, 462 F. Supp. 3d 572
    (D. Md., 2020), https://www.leagle.com/decision/infdco20200524n63.

35 U.S. Federal Labor Relations Authority, 71 FLRA 1223, 71 FLRA 1235, https://
    www.flra.gov/authority_decisions_volumes/71.

36 U.S. Federal Labor Relations Authority, 71 FLRA No. 232, Patent Office
    Professional Association (Union) and United States Patent and Trademark
    Office, Alexandria, Virginia (Agency), https://www.flra.gov/decisions/v71/71-
    232.html; 71 FLRA No. 233, National Treasury Employees Union (Union) and
    United States Patent and Trademark Office (Agency), https://www.flra.gov/
    decisions/v71/71-233.html.

37 James Sherk, "Tales from the Swamp," America First Policy, February 1, 2021,
    https://americafirstpolicy.com/assets/uploads/files/Tales_from_the_swamp.
    pdf.

38 Exec. Order 13957, October 21, 2020, "Creating Schedule F in the Excepted
    Service," 85 Fed. Reg. 67631 (October 26, 2020), https://www.govinfo.gov/
    content/pkg/FR-2020-10-26/pdf/2020-23780.pdf.

39 American Federation of Government Employees, "Trump Administration's
    Order to Expand Excepted Service Opens Door to Political Cronyism,
    Largest Federal Employee Union Says," Press Release, October 22, 2020,

https://www.afge.org/publication/trump-administrations-order-to-expand-excepted-service-opens-door-to-political-cronyism-largest-federal-employee-union-says/.

40 Erich Wagner, "'Stunning' Executive Order Would Politicize Civil Service," *Government Executive*, October 22, 2020, https://www.govexec.com/management/2020/10/stunning-executive-order-would-politicize-civil-service/169479/.

41 Sherk, "Tales from the Swamp."

42 Exec. Order 14003, January 22, 2021, "Protecting the Federal Workforce," 86 Fed. Reg. 7231 (January 27, 2021), https://www.federalregister.gov/documents/2021/01/27/2021-01924/protecting-the-federal-workforce.

43 Sherk, "Tales from the Swamp."

44 U.S. Office of Personnel Management, *2021 Federal Employee Viewpoint Survey Results*, April 28, 2022, https://www.opm.gov/fevs/reports/governmentwide-reports/governmentwide-management-report/governmentwide-report/2021/2021-governmentwide-management-report.pdf.

45 Sherk, "Tales from the Swamp."

46 Tracy Stone-Manning, Email to Headquarters Staff and Executive Leadership Team, Re: Headquarters duty stations in Washington DC and Grand Junction CO, September 7, 2022.

47 Scott Streater, "Union wants to negotiate BLM headquarters' return to D.C.: The union's bargaining request clearly shows that not all headquarters employees are on board with BLM Director Tracy Stone-Manning's plan to move dozens of staffers from Grand Junction, Colo, back to Washington," *Greenwire*, September 9, 2022.

48 U.S. Office of Personnel Management, *2021 Federal Employee Viewpoint Survey Results*, 12.

49 Exec. Order 14058, December 13, 2021, "Transforming Federal Customer Experience and Service Delivery to Rebuild Trust in Government," 86 Fed. Reg. 71357 (December 16, 2021), https://www.govinfo.gov/content/pkg/FR-2021-12-16/pdf/2021-27380.pdf.

50 U.S. Department of the Interior, *A Report to the President, 2017–2021*, January 15, 2021, https://www.doi.gov/sites/doi.gov/files/a-report-to-the-president-u.s.-department-of-the-interior-2017-2021.pdf.

51 U.S. Department of Transportation, "Administrative Rulemaking, Guidance, and Enforcement Procedures," 84 Fed. Reg. 71714 (December 27, 2019), https://www.federalregister.gov/documents/2019/12/27/2019-26672/administrative-rulemaking-guidance-and-enforcement-procedures.

52 Ibid., 71729.

53 Ibid., 71716.

54 Ibid.

55 Ibid.

56 Ibid., 71732.

57 Council on Environmental Quality, "Update to the Regulations Implementing the Procedural Provisions of the National Environmental Policy Act," 85 Fed. Reg. 43304 (July 16, 2020), https://www.federalregister.gov/documents/2020/07/16/2020-15179/update-to-the-regulations-implementing-the-procedural-provisions-of-the-national-environmental.

58 Early Participation in Regulations Act of 2019, S.1419, 116th Cong. (2019–2020), https://www.congress.gov/bill/116th-congress/senate-bill/1419.

59 Setting Manageable Analysis Requirements in Text (SMART) Act of 2021, S.2801, 117th Cong. (2021–2022), https://www.congress.gov/bill/117th-congress/senate-bill/2801.

60 Regulations from the Executive in Need of Scrutiny Act of 2021, S.68, 117th Cong. (2021–2022), https://www.congress.gov/bill/117th-congress/senate-bill/68/.

61 Regulatory Accountability Act, S.2278, 117th Cong. (2021–2022), https://www.congress.gov/bill/117th-congress/senate-bill/2278.

62 Small Business Regulatory Flexibility Improvements Act, S.1120, 116th Cong. (2019–2020), https://www.congress.gov/bill/116th-congress/senate-bill/1120.

63 SCRUB Act, H.R.998, 115th Cong. (2017–2018), https://www.congress.gov/bill/115th-congress/house-bill/998.

CHAPTER 8—DRIVING CHANGE AS A POLITICAL EMPLOYEE

1 Morrison v. Olson, 487 U.S. 654 (1988), https://supreme.justia.com/cases/federal/us/487/654/.

2 Alan B. Morrison, "The Principal Officer Puzzle," *Yale Journal on Regulation*, Notice and Comment, November 15, 2019, https://www.yalejreg.com/nc/the-principal-officer-puzzle-by-alan-b-morrison/.

3 The Secretary of the Interior, Order No. 3395, "Temporary Suspension of Delegated Authority," U.S. Department of the Interior, January 20, 2021, https://www.akleg.gov/basis/get_documents.asp?docid=7.

4 Steven Nelson, "Anchors away! Biden purges Trump appointees from Naval, Air Force academies, West Point," *New York Post*, September 8, 2021, https://nypost.com/2021/09/08/biden-fires-trump-trio-from-naval-academy-board/.

5 Emma Dumain and Jennifer Yachnin, "3 takeaways from Deb Haaland's Senate appearance," *E&E News*, July 28, 2021, https://www.eenews.net/articles/3-takeaways-from-deb-haalands-senate-appearance/.

6 U. S. Department of the Interior, Office of Inspector General, "Reassignment of Senior Executives at U.S. Department of the Interior," Report No. 2017-ER-061, April 2018.

7 5 U.S.C. § 3131.

INDEX